THE OLD AQUEDUCT IN QUERÉTARO

OLD MOTHER MEXICO

BY
HARRY CARR

With Illustrations by
LOUIS H. RUYL

Boston and New York
HOUGHTON MIFFLIN COMPANY
The Riverside Press Cambridge

917.2
C 230
70299
June, 1970

The Riverside Press
CAMBRIDGE · MASSACHUSETTS
PRINTED IN THE U.S.A.

CONTENTS

iv CONTENTS

ILLUSTRATIONS

OLD MOTHER MEXICO

∴

CHAPTER I

OLD MOTHER MEXICO

MEXICO is the mother of our West. She gave us our earliest heroes. The historic shrines of the Mexican West Coast are also our historic shrines.

It is often said that the West began in the rough little frontier towns in the valleys of the Mississippi — Council Bluffs and Kansas City — from which the first covered wagons started on the long trek across the country of the buffalo and the Indians.

The story of the West really began in a sleepy little sun-drenched town on the West Coast of Mexico two hundred years before the Indians looked down from their signal peaks to see the first covered wagons jolting along in the buffalo trails. The West began with a gay young Spanish cavalier who was searching for seven fabled cities where the houses were built with walls of gold. Young Coronado didn't find the Seven Golden Cities of Cibola — but he discovered the West.

The eastern part of the United States was pioneered by the Pilgrim Fathers who were seeking to escape from persecution in Europe. They were followed by sober-minded folk, seeking investments, homes, and opportunities. The West was settled by adventurers who were looking for the end of the rainbow. They were always led on by

the will-o'-the-wisp of high adventure. There is nothing
for which people will dare so much or suffer so horribly as
the pursuit of a romantic dream.

One dismal rain-soaked day in March, 1930, I set out
from California with a party of engineers in a cavalcade of
automobiles. They were to map a highway down the West
Coast of Mexico. I was on the way to discover the places
where our West began; to find the forgotten heroes of this
dramatic chapter of our history. Wild storms were sweeping over the jagged peaks of the Sierra Madres when we
arrived at Nogales. We had to put our five little cars —
equipped for camping — in a garage and wait for a week
for the rain to wear itself out.

Meanwhile I found Nogales interesting. For untold
centuries it has been the gateway to our great Southwest.
It has been soaked with blood and decorated with lurid
adventure. Nestling in a pass of the mysterious desert
mountains, it has seen strange prehistoric people — naked
ape-like savages — shuffling through on their way to the
warm lush lands of the South. It has seen the coming of
Spanish knights and their men-at-arms with their big bell-
muzzled guns and their seven-ply deerskin armor; prospectors searching for gold — pioneers in covered wagons.
Its rock-walled cañons have echoed to the yells of cruel
Apaches who swooped down from the hills — killing,
burning, destroying.

There can be little doubt that Nogales lies along the
route of the 'first people'... the mother race. They must
have come this way because there was no other way. So I
imagine that the first man who walked through this mountain gateway was Ug. I call him Ug because I am sure that
he had a name that sounded like a grunt.

He was a dirty savage who lived in the desolate wastes of Siberia. He must have been a daring soul — and one filled with curiosity. He squatted on his heels on a Siberian rock and wondered what was in that dim blue line of mountains he could see as he looked across the cold Arctic waters to the storm-swept shores of Alaska. He had to find out or 'bust!' His curiosity was just eating him up!

It is possible that there was at that time a causeway of rock that he crossed. I think he came in a boat. He made a boat out of the trunk of a tree — or maybe of the skins of wild animals — and fought his way across the wild waters to the shores of North America. The other wild people sat around and wondered what had become of Ug until they couldn't stand it any longer. They had to go and find out. I doubt if there was any great general trek. No general migration. At least at first. I think one or two daring souls followed Ug; then a few families slipped across on a calm day, and so on.

America was started.

They landed in Alaska and found it very cold; so they turned south and wandered on and on for thousands of years. Ug died, but his children went on. So it may be that Ug's great-great-great-great-great-great-grandson's great-great-great-great-great-great-grandson was the first to see Nogales. At that, I fear I have left out a large collection of great-great-grandsons. It was a period of thousands of years. Nobody knows how many thousands. Anyhow, Ug's remote descendants wandered down through what is now Oregon and California — on until they came to Mexico. By the time they had come into the sunlit valleys of Mexico and the thick jungles of Central America, they had become wise and cultured and did not feed so many fleas. They built great empires and beautiful temples.

I have found their footsteps. In Coachella Valley in California is a mute record of one of their age-old tragedies. Making their way south, they stopped for breathing spells that probably lasted for centuries. One of these breathing spells was in Coachella Valley — now one of the great winter resorts of the world, where the celebrities come to boil out at Palm Springs.

You can see their story written on a great rock headland on the border between Riverside and Imperial Counties. They were probably living in a fertile valley and were perhaps learning to raise crops, when the sea suddenly began rushing in upon them... a mighty flood like the flood of Noah in the Bible. They saw destruction coming and carved into the rock thousands of frantic prayers, begging their heathen gods to save them.

But the heathen gods did not save them. The waters came in and probably destroyed them. You can see where the wild surf lashed the rock sixty or seventy feet above the place where they carved their prayers. The sea stayed there for a long time. Scientists estimate that the waters buried those pitiful prayers for twenty-five thousand years. Then the sea went out again, leaving their rock carvings again on the floor of the desert. It is the earliest recorded tragedy of the Wild West.

At the other end of the valley — not far from the winter colony where the movie stars and other famous people have their desert homes — is another mark of another tragedy. The same lashing sea which destroyed one prehistoric people when it rushed in, destroyed another prehistoric people when it went away. On the side of a desert hill near the present town of Indio is a series of fish-traps — circles of rock with a little gateway to let in the unwary fish. There are seven series of these fish-traps sagging down the hill, showing how the fishers had to build new traps as the waters began to recede. The last trap is almost on the floor of the desert. There are of course various theories of various scientists as to these rock markings, some flatly contradicting this explanation.

As Ug shuffled along through Nogales, some of his people must have dropped out of the procession and stayed behind to become the Apaches. Most of the early tragedies of the West — both before and after the covered wagons came — have been Apache tragedies.

This was always their country. For various reasons, too long to explain here, I am convinced that the Apaches and their cousins the Navajos were the last people to come across from Siberia. To this day the mark of the Mongol is plainly written upon them — in their speech, their customs, and their appearance.

It is always with a feeling of incensed resentment that I hear French criminals from the slums of Paris spoken of as 'Apaches.' Our Apaches of the Southwest were cruel and merciless. They defended their country from white invaders with the ferocity of wild wolves. But they were — and are — a remarkable people. White men who have lived among them admire them for their sense of honor, for their courage, and for their brains. The agent who now rules them in the name of our Uncle Sam says that not even the Sioux or the Cheyenne were as high a type of men. Major Frederick Burnham, who is the most famous scout of modern times, tells me that the Apache was the greatest fighting man — the finest natural soldier — who ever lived in any land or at any period of history. He could go days on end without food or water. He could run alongside a horse until the horse dropped dead from exhaustion. Encumbered with women and children, an Apache tribe has been known to travel seventy-five miles in a single night. In a country where a white man starved for food and sank down, crazed with thirst, his tongue hanging, black and swollen from his mouth, the Apache lived high. He knew the secrets of the desert. The barrel cactus gave him water. He found food in many desert plants. Also his liquor.

The Apache was a past-master of military strategy. Our West-Pointers were ignorant children in his hands. During our fiercest war against the Apaches we had five thousand of our finest regular troops in the field for years. The Apaches under Geronimo numbered never more than thirty-eight — many of whom were young boys. But our soldiers never could cope with them until they hired a rival band of Apaches to fight them at so much per day's work. Even then old Geronimo was never beaten. He finally quit because he got tired of fighting. Fine irony that the other Apaches always sniffed with scorn at Geronimo because he was not really a war chief — only a medicine-man — sort of soapbox orator.

My Apache friends tell me that the white man was always easy to beat because he did not understand the laws of mind over matter. The explanation they gave me was so difficult to understand that I had to hang on by the handles not to sink clear under. Suffice it to say that the throb-throb of the Apache war drum is there to establish a rhythm which produces certain psychic conditions which are not taught at West Point.

I have often asked my Apache friends how it was that their old warriors could have been so tiger cruel and yet so courageous. They gave me a typical Apache answer. 'We used to tie our captives to the stake and start to burn them. When the fire began to leap up around them, we watched their faces. If they did not show fear, we turned them loose and let them go. If their faces showed fear, we knew they were just trash, and trash ought to be burned.'

At the same time, there are many elements in the process of being held head down over a fire that singes your hair off and parches your face that do not contribute to complete *sang-froid* or mental equanimity. There were not many who did not show symptoms of nervousness.

You can see that the Spanish knights and explorers who came wandering up from the West Coast of Mexico, looking for gold cities, had their hands pretty full in the matter of fighting.

The charm of exploring this old gateway to the West is that it remains in many essentials as it was in the past. Nogales is, in reality, twins. A chicken-wire fence separates a modern up-to-date American border town from changeless, mysterious Mexico. On the Mexican side, Nogales is colorful and picturesque — old men in cotton pants walking along sidewalks carrying little tables on their heads. The tables are covered with candy — dulces — made of cactus and protected by netting to keep off the flies. It is a sort of gluggy paste and tastes something like Turkish candy. Mexican women selling tortillas and enchiladas cooked on tin stoves in the gutters, light streaming into the pungent chile-scented darkness from saloon doors; soldiers, lovely slim-legged girls in shabby mourning (in Mexico one wears mourning for distant rela-

tives); American cabarets; tourists buying post-cards; the
soft strum of guitars; meandering burros; the hoot and
rush of motor cars. The streets used to be lined with beggars. Of late years, however, the town has been cleaned
up by progressive Mexican officials. Good for progress,
but bad for romance. I miss the old women who held out
their withered brown hands for alms and murmured sadly,
'God will reward you, senor.' Once in a while in Mexican
Nogales you see a man of the mountains, strayed in from
fastnesses that few men dare to explore. We saw one
strange-looking fellow. He was in rags and tatters, with
long unkempt hair and a beard straggling over his face.
He wore an old-fashioned cloak that might have been
worn in the Middle Ages by Don Quixote.

A proof of the strength of the British Empire is that
Providence allows the English to pronounce Don Quixote
— that musical Don Kee-hoe-tay — as though it were
Quicks-ot — and still does not sink the British Islands
into the sea as punishment. Spanish is the loveliest and
most murdered of all languages. The sweetest sound I
know in any language is the name Juan; not Wah-n, but
Juan breathed like a little caress. The rhyme of Lord
Byron's 'Don Juan' proves that he called the name
'Jew-Ann.' Any poet who can write a deathless romance
about anyone named Jew-Ann must have a high-powered
imagination or a defective ear-pan — or both. Probably
both.

One of the historic places in Nogales is an old cave.
It is bored in under a hill that has been pelted and torn
by bullets and shell-fire. Once the cave was a prison and
it must have been a very cold one. Now it is a café where
you eat venison from the hills and marvelous fish foods

from the Gulf of California. As you eat, street musicians
come wandering in. One is a wan young man with a
bullet scar on his cheek. He carries a time-stained violin.
The 'cello-player is a sad-eyed old man in shabby clothes.
A fat boy plays a huge guitar upon whose stained wood is
painted a rose. The fat boy keeps nodding off to sleep,
but by some miracle never misses a note.

The barkeeper feels a host's responsibility for our entertainment. Wiping a glass, he gestures, with both the glass
and the towel in his eagerness to tell the musicians to
play the lovely *Estrellita* for us. He joins in when they
play *Cielito Lindo*, and comes around from the bar to
urge them to play *Amapola del Camino* for *los Americanos*.
He says it is a so-lovely little song about a little flower
that grows by the roadside.

We were sorry to leave Nogales as our little caravan
passed through the gate in the chicken-wire fence. We
were always sorry to leave every town that we saw.
Mexico is a land of sweetness and charm — as well as
tragedy and tears. It grips your heart.

The astonishing thing about Mexico is the cinema-like
suddenness of the changes. You roll along a town street
in Nogales — the cabaret roadhouse, the placid-looking
brewery, a battalion of troops drilling by the roadside.
As though someone had shifted the scenery, you are in the
heart of a foreign country. Half-ruined long adobes that
look like abandoned barracks, quaint little ranches, a
burro standing in philosophical meditation, perhaps a cow
or a couple of goats, huts made half of stone and half of
adobe, corrals built sometimes of stone, sometimes of the
wands of ocotillo cactus growing in a close network. We
pass one forlorn little ranch that crowds in toward the

road. At one end of the corral is a tiny tower of stone and adobe to keep the grain safe from the wood rats. The Mexican Indians had silos centuries before our farmers ever heard of them.

As we roll along the road, the ceaseless life of Mexico flows by. Two or three fierce-looking cowboys ride by, driving a bunch of half-wild long-horned cattle in from the ranges back in the hills. The cowboys are draped with cartridge belts and guns, but lift their big sombreros courteously as they pass.

The Mexican cowboy is a type remote from ours. He wears an enormous sombrero and sometimes tight leather trousers. His spurs are as big as saucers. It is a fact not generally known that the first cowboys in America were Spanish soldiers who had served their time in the army and had been discharged. They began to herd cattle at San Diego, California. They invented the stock saddle and the lasso and most of the cowboy paraphernalia — two hundred years before an American cowboy saw the prairies. They evolved the cowboy saddle from the old Moorish war-saddles they had seen in Spain.

The cow-saddle of the Mexican vaquero is quite different from the stock saddles of our cowboys. It lies low and flat. The pommel is as big as a dish and tilts backward toward the rider. In some parts of Mexico the cowboys wear the 'chaps' of our Southern cowboys — hair pants. Farther south, they have a wide leather blanket that falls on either side of the horse's shoulders from the saddle pommel. In rough country, the rider spreads the ends of this blanket back over his legs and knees to protect them from the underbrush. It is just as effective as 'chaps' and not so hot.

The Mexican cow-ponies are small and tough, with tiny hard hoofs. They are descendants of the Arab war-horses brought over from Spain by the Spanish knights with Cortes. They lack the strength and power of our larger cattle-horses. As a consequence, the Mexican cow-boy seldom rides as well as the American, but he is a better roper. There used to be a saying on the old California cattle ranges that a Mexican vaquero could throw a lasso better with his feet than a Gringo with his hands. There is — and was — a reason. The Mexican cattle run in the thick chaparral and they go like scared deer. There is neither time nor room to use the wide loops of our cow-hands. The Mexican throws a small loop and it goes like a bullet.

The endless burro trains — burros loaded with wood, burros almost hidden under huge bundles of hay, one lone sad-looking woman driving two burros loaded with pottery, burros carrying peons whose long legs almost touch the ground on either side. We passed one tiny burro surmounted by a huge cow-saddle which in turn was topped by a very fat man with a big sombrero and a machete. He had the portentous look of a knight of the Round Table out on a search for adventure and achievement.

We never grew tired of looking at the burros. The burro is the pack-horse, the express wagon, and the philosophical friend of Mexico. It would be impossible for Mexico to live without him. His strength is incredible. We saw burros ambling along in uncomplaining placidity with such enormous loads that all we could see were four little feet. If one of our heavy draft horses could carry a load as big in proportion to his weight, he could walk off with a house.

One day we were waiting at a railroad siding when a

Mexican came along with a tiny fawn-colored burrito.
We did not know that the peon spoke English. He was
very fat. 'Do you suppose,' I said to one of the engineers,
'that this hippopotamus is going to ride on that mouse?'
The peon gave no sign that he understood. But when he
had cinched up the saddle, he said, with dignified gravity,
'Come here, mouse. The hippopotamus is going to ride
you.'

We were in barefoot land now. We were to see very few
shoes from this on. The Mexican peon wears loose white
cotton pants that he rolls up over his knees on occasion,
a long loose cotton shirt like a Russian blouse, and a huge
straw sombrero. For shoes he has sandals called *guarachas*.

The Mexicans are a very appealing people. Generous,
kind. Their courtesy is unfailing. When we met them
along the road, they would take off their sombreros and
say, 'Buenos dias, señor.' Or sometimes they would say
'Adios' — which means both 'How-do-you-do' and 'Good-
bye' to the Mexican. Once in a while we would meet one
extra polite who said, 'Vaya con Dios, señor' (Go with
God, sir.)

For a long time it puzzled us why they should say
'good-nights' and 'good-days' instead of 'good-night'
and 'good-day,' until we realized that 'Buenas noches' is
an abbreviation of a phrase meaning 'God give you good
nights'... not to be stingy with the good measure.

CHAPTER II

QUICKSAND

WE had an adventure with quicksand that first day out. Having wriggled our way through a narrow, twisty cañon heavily timbered with cottonwood and sycamore, we came down a hill and into a broad valley. The tiny Magdalena River — swollen by rains — was chattering and scolding as it hurried over the rocks. We should have known that trouble waited ahead when we saw two patient peons with their teams on the far side of the river. But our foremost car went grunting and snorting into the middle of a bed of quicksand. There it stuck, with the river purling over the running-boards.

One of the peons drove his team into the river and hitched on to the front of the car. The team consisted of two forlorn scrubby little broncos. They struggled vainly. But each of the broncos had his own ideas and they couldn't get themselves going at the same time — or in the same direction. Then the other peon hitched on his team. He had a sad-looking bronco and a little white mule. That mule had a way of smiling to himself over a little joke of his own. I am afraid he did not really love his art. His heart was not in the business of dragging that car out of the quicksand. The peons shouted diabolic cries; two or three little Mexican boys waded into the river and tried to push on the wheels, but the car stuck. In the end, the engineers had to rig up a block and tackle which they made fast to a tree-stump. With that and the

help of two or three other cars, the automobile finally
came out of the quicksand with gluggy, sucking noises.
The little white mule kept smiling to himself.

As always in Mexico we found contrasts — the oldest
cheek by jowl with the newest — the cruelest with the
most saintly. Thus we found the historic footprints of
Mexico's noblest and Mexico's worst adventurer — Father
Eusebio Kino and Pancho Villa.

The bleak, mysterious mountains of Sonora and the
deserts have produced some of the most extraordinary
men of the New World. In the days of the Spanish Conquest, Sonora was the far-distant frontier — like our
Montana or the Dakotas of the frontier days. The strong
men ruled. So from Sonora came Father Kino, Father
Garces, Juan Bautista de Anza, and in latter days Calles,
Pancho Villa, Colonel Emilio Kosterlitzsky. Divers types
of divers standards of morals, but men of strength and
high adventure.

Kosterlitzsky, born in a Russian Cossack camp, Mexican
by adoption, had organized a company of sentenced con-
victs into the famous rurales who policed northern Mexico
with a rod of iron. In the days of his power he once had a
horseback duel with Pancho Villa which did not end
until they had fired their revolvers empty and threw the
empty guns at each other. Brave old Kosterlitzsky, who
once put down a mutiny of a battalion of troops by shouting orders at an imaginary regiment as he rode up to the
riotous garrison alone.

Pancho had whirled through this part of Mexico like a
Hun destroyer of the Middle Ages. We passed old adobe
barracks wrecked by his gun-fire; ranch after ranch that
he had looted. Like Captain Kidd he left innumerable

legends of buried treasure. Every few months someone
gets up an expedition in Hollywood to find the treasure-
troves of the murderous Villa. Pancho was a very peculiar
character — ignorant, wise, shrewd, cruel, and sometimes
strangely just. A leader absolutely uneducated in the art
of soldiering, yet a great soldier. One minute he was
found helping the poor and needy; the next executing
someone who had offended him by a chance remark.
We passed through one little town that had suffered cruelly
at his hands. He had demanded money of the business
men. One insisted that he had no money. Pancho
promptly shot him. 'But,' protested one of his officers,
'he really had no money. I know the man well. He
hasn't two pesos to jingle against each other.' 'Sure,'
answered Pancho shrewdly. 'That's why I shot him. I
wanted to show the others that I wasn't fooling. Why
should I shoot one that really had money hidden — who
could be made to tell?'

During his most disastrous campaign, Villa's army
passed across the great Cananea cattle-ranch below Naco.
Instead of resisting, the manager of the ranch rode through
the rebel lines and asked Villa frankly how many steers
he needed for his army — knowing that they would be
taken anyhow. Pancho designated the number and they
were delivered — all neatly butchered by the stock hands
of the ranch. Pancho — pleased — promised that no more
stock should be taken.

In a savage little battle that went into history as
'shots were exchanged across the line,' Pancho was badly
shot up by United States troops at Nogales. Afterward
the Federal troops of the Mexican army gave him a
terrible licking. Starving, weak, faint, and exhausted, his

defeated army went back the way it came. When they got back to the Cananea ranch, his troops were dropping in their tracks from hunger. Yet — true to his word — he would not allow his starving men to take a single steer. His word was good.

Near the marks of the ruin wrought by this marauder, we found the lovely old church from which Father Kino started many of his famous explorations. Father Kino was one of the most heroic figures of the drama of our early West, yet his name has been forgotten. Few east of the Rio Grande have ever heard of him. He discovered the West.

Eusebio Kino was born in Austria. He was a scientist and a mathematician. When about forty years old, he became very ill. Everyone thought he would die. He made a pledge to God that if his life were spared, he would spend the remainder of his days doing missionary work among the Indians of Mexico. After he was well again, his friends wanted him to forget it and to accept a high position as a professor of mathematics in a great university in Europe. But he kept his word.

Father Kino came to Mexico about the year 1680. If he had lived in our day, we should have called him a 'go-getter.' A man of furious, indomitable energy, stern, severe — a scientific, cultured, determined man in a day of wild adventurers. He built some fifty missions in northern Mexico and Arizona; made fifteen journeys of exploration. More than a century before Frémont — the Pathfinder — crossed the plains, Father Kino had explored the Southwest. And exploring was no joke in those days. The country was infested by merciless wild Apaches who swept down from the hills like ferocious wolves, torturing, destroying. The desert was scarcely less dangerous than the Indians. Long waterless stretches of aching heat. Sometimes with an escort, sometimes alone, Father Kino mapped and explored the desert. As an explorer one of his most remarkable feats was the discovery — largely a matter of scientific deduction — that California was fastened to the main land. Most of the early sea voyages were made on the theory that California was an island; the early voyages were for the purpose of finding the Northwest Passage around the end of it. Father Kino ended that long-drawn-out dream.

Many legends have come down of him. It is related that one of his exploring trips through Arizona was interrupted by a runner who told him that the Spanish officers were about to execute one of his faithful Indian converts. Father Kino turned back, rode a hundred and fifty miles as fast as his saddle mule could travel, and arrived in time to place himself in front of the firing squad and defy them to shoot.

One of his loveliest missions is in the old town of San Ignacio to which we came presently. It was the first of the rural towns we saw. Nogales is a railroad center and port of entry. San Ignacio was a little sleepy country town with the sun beating down on adobe walls. Nobody seemed to be doing anything. A few burros wandered around the streets, peons squatting in the doorways. Here and there in the shade of a ramada, a woman was patting tortillas. And standing over the town this splendid old church. Many historians contend that Father Kino is buried under its altars. In the shadows of its walls are three or four old brick tombs in which priests lie buried; but the weight of facts seem to indicate that

Father Kino lies under the altars of Magdalena — another mission town.

No one knows the age of the old church at San Ignacio. It was probably built about the year 1690. You can see the influence of the Moorish conquerors of Spain in the domes and the winding caracol stairways. We could not understand how the workmen ever got those heavy blocks of stone in place without modern hoisting machinery.

One of the bells in the old belfry is broken — a big chunk bitten out of the side. It may have been broken by some early sexton who got excited over the marriage of the beautiful village belle and put too much steam into the ringing. I am afraid, however, it was smashed by a bullet in some forgotten revolution. Every church in Mexico has experienced its tragedies.

Inside the church a class of little Mexican children were saying their lessons to a very pretty and very dignified young señorita who had a lovely name — Maria Teresa Gallegos (pronounced Gah-yay-gos). She showed us the old wooden images that were made long, long ago by the Indians. One was a figure of Jesus Christ. The Indian women had put a dress with a frilled skirt that stood out like a ballet-dancer's upon His naked body. The figure of the saint that we call John the Baptist, but whom the Mexicans call San Juan Bautista, wore a baby's dress. No doubt this lovely little garment of fine drawn-work linen had been made by some little Indian mother whose baby had been saved from death by her prayers.

One of the relics at San Ignacio was a very old Bible whose leaves were yellow with age. Inside the cover were these words written in a beautiful penmanship with old-fashioned flourishes: 'Ay por Dios rezen un padre por eterna descanzo de mi alma.' It means, 'For the love of God, pray an Our Father [the name of a prayer] for the eternal peace of my soul.' I imagine that it must have been written there by someone whose troubles seemed to him more than he could bear — a soul worn with sorrow.

Maria Teresa smiled when I told her, and related a little story that had been told to her by her nurse. A man afflicted like this one of the Bible inscription had a cross that seemed too heavy for him to bear. One night he had a dream — only he was never convinced that it was a dream. In the dream, Jesus Christ came to him with deep sympathy. 'Come with me,' He said. 'If your cross is heavier than you can carry.' He led the sorrowing man to a pit in which were thrown thousands of crosses — huge crosses of timbers, little crosses, middle-sized crosses. Among the other crosses, the man saw a tiny, tiny cross. When Jesus told him that he might choose his own cross from the heap, he asked timidly, 'Might I take this little tiny bit of a one? Is that asking too much, Lord?' Jesus smiled benignly. 'That,' He said, 'is the one you are now carrying.'

We had luncheon that day in a very ancient town called Santa Ana. It is a place rich with history. At one time it was a center — a trading-post for the mines. When Mexico belonged to Spain, the King handed out tracts of land to his favorites. On some of the lands were ledges of gold. But the Spaniards did not claw out the ore with the feverish haste that we always do. They didn't hurry about anything. They figured that it had been there for a long time and wasn't likely to run away. Anyhow, there was another reason. When a Spanish grandee found gold on his land, he regarded it as selfish and stingy to take out all the gold for himself. He regarded his gold mine as a bank account for his children and his grandchildren. He took out only enough gold to pay his expenses.

At the time of the revolution against Spain, the old grandees could not believe that the imperial banners were being lowered forever. They felt sure that some day the rebels would be properly punished and they would come back to rule. So they carefully closed their gold mines. They cunningly closed the entrances to the old shafts. For a hundred years, prospectors have been looking for those lost Spanish mines. Sometimes they find the ore dumps, but very seldom have they been able to find the mines. Whatever else may be said about them, the Spanish were clever people — great engineers and architects.

We drove into Santa Ana and found a stuffy little house back of a saloon, where we had luncheon. Among other things the señora brought us a sort of stew made of jerked beef. I had often read in old accounts how explorers lived on 'jerky.' It is made by cutting beef into strips and hanging it up to dry in the sun. It tastes all right, but it involves a lot of work. It is like eating a lasso. Gladstone, the great English statesman, said that he always chewed everything thirty times. Thirty chews wouldn't have given him even a good start had he been eating venison jerky. If the Mexican people have been raised on jerky, I don't wonder that they never hurry. A luncheon on jerky is a job for the afternoon. Luckily, we also had tortillas, which are little flat corn cakes beaten so thin by the hands of the Mexican women that they are almost like tissue paper. Sometimes, in fact, the women pin them up on the walls until they are needed.

Everywhere you go in Mexico you see the women slap-

ping hunks of corn dough from one hand to the other —
patting the tortillas thin. Once an enterprising American
thought he would make the meals of the natives more
sanitary by inventing a machine to pat tortillas. He built
a big factory. It now stands idle. His customers com-
plained that the tortillas lacked 'el savor de mano' (the
flavor of the hand).

We drove all that night across the empty, desolate
plains of northern Mexico. At four o'clock in the morning, we rolled into the beautiful city of Hermosillo. We
knew it must be a beautiful place because the name
means 'little beautiful one.' But nothing looks beautiful
to anyone at four o'clock in the morning — with a
stomach so empty it feels like a cistern.

The police force turned out to meet us. Mexican police-
men are very polite and dignified. They met us and routed
out the proprietor of a Chinese café to give us something
to eat. All Chinese cooks are workers in magic. No
matter what the hour or what the emergency, they are
never dismayed. I have seen a party of ten suddenly and
without warning descend upon a lonely vaquero camp in
the middle of a wilderness; but the Chinese cook always
had a five-course dinner ready. The Chinese café proprietor was unruffled, but the police were panic-stricken
because they couldn't find a taxi to take us to the restau-
rant. We insisted — to their frozen horror — on riding to
the café in the police patrol wagon. They were really
agonized with shame when they shut us up in the wire
cage. The driver simply tore through the quiet streets.
He wanted to get the dreadful ordeal over as soon as
possible. I imagine that the Hermosillo police force still
gets gooseflesh at the memory of the crazy Gringos who

insisted on riding to breakfast in the 'Black Maria.' Full of beefsteak, ham and eggs, and coffee, we fairly staggered into bed, leaving the police sergeant telling the hotel clerk in a hoarse whisper the terrible mortification that had befallen the city.

CHAPTER III

A MEXICAN ROOSEVELT

IT seemed as though we had just hit our pillows when an excited Mexican hammered on our doors and informed us that the Governor of the great State of Sonora had come to call on us. At the moment we were tempted to tell the Governor of the great State of Sonora to go jump in the lake. But we finally crawled sleepily out of bed and pulled on our clothes.

In the end we were glad, for the Governor turned out to be a fine fellow. He made us think of Roosevelt. Until he got to be Governor, Francisco Elias was a cattleman — one of the great cattle barons of Mexico. He still owns one of the largest cattle-ranches in the world. He is never so happy as when he is in the saddle on top of a bronco — the wilder the better.

The Governor — unlike many other governors I have known — did not try to be impressive. He took us to ride in his own car and drove it himself. And when the Governor drives, you had better hang on tight. He may have heard the rumor that an automobile can go slower than sixty miles an hour, but apparently never found out by trying. The Governor's favorite remark was 'O.K. Let's go.' And Go meant Go with him. Perhaps the best index to the Governor's character is that all the people call him 'Pancho,' which is a pet name for Francisco — just as we call the Richard we are fond of, 'Dick.'

When it got hot, Pancho took off his coat and drove in

his shirt-sleeves. Once a workman on the road flagged him down, as it were, and rode a few miles with us to the place where his job called him. Several times the Governor stopped the car and got out to show a road foreman how to manage a new road machine — lately imported from the United States. During our long ride through Mexico we came into intimate touch with many governors. Almost without exception, they were remarkable men — men who would have been recognized as outstanding figures in any country and in any kind of work. It is they who are making the new Mexico.

Governor 'Pancho' drove us in his car to many interesting places, two of which should be seen by every American because they mean much to our own history.

One was an old mill at a place called Los Angeles — like our California city. This mill was very beautiful — which most mills are not. Low adobe buildings surrounding a great plaza; a lovely Mexican house where the manager of the mill lived; large cool rooms with windows peering like little tunnels through adobe walls four feet thick. We had luncheon in a room that opened into a patio fragrant with rose blossoms. We had many delightful dishes I had known before — one or two of which I had never heard. One was tomatoes stuffed with baby shrimps. After you have eaten that, you could well place a silver memorial plate on your tum-tum, close it up, and stop eating forever more, sure that you will never find anything else as good.

The cotton-mill itself is so old that no one knows its age. Centuries before the first white men saw Mexico, the present city of Hermosillo was an Indian village. The Indians who lived there were called Seris. At that time the Aztecs were building a great empire in the southern part of Mexico. They wished to extend their sway and power. So they tried to make friends with other native peoples far to the North. They had an idea of founding something like our modern league of nations. They sent a delegation on a long and terrible journey across the mountains and rivers, from the South of Mexico where the remains of the Aztec ruins can still be seen, to the land of the Seris. They brought with them many presents — no doubt, rugs and cloaks made of feathers woven together into cloth. The important gift they brought — as it turned out — were the seeds of a plant of which the Seris had never heard — cotton. They showed the Seris how to plant the cotton seeds and how to weave the cotton into cloth.

From that day to this, this old town of Los Angeles has been a cotton mill. From time to time the crude looms have been changed. The skilled hands of the Indian women gave way to water power with a huge wooden water wheel that still stands there. Water power served its day and gave way to steam which now runs the old mill, turning out fifty thousand yards of cotton cloth a day. Which would have surprised the old Seris and Aztecs a good deal.

From Los Angeles we drove to another ancient town called San Miguel Horcasitas. Here was the cradle in which our modern West was born. It should be such a shrine of our history as Plymouth Rock.

It was from San Miguel Horcasitas that the gallant Captain Juan Bautista de Anza started with the first band of settlers who ever crossed the plains to California. This was the year of our Revolutionary War and about sixty years before the first covered wagons of those whom we call the pioneers and the pathfinders. De Anza crossed the plains and founded the city of San Francisco. Most important of all, he brought the first pioneer women, the pioneer mothers. And with them, civilization.

Parenthetically I might remark that civilization never sticks until the women come. The conquering flag of civilization has always been the baby's diaper hanging on the clothesline. What does history say? Long ago, the Norsemen came with their wassail bowls and their fierce two-handed swords. They breasted the storms of the North Sea and found their way to the shores of America. Somewhere up in the cold winds of New Brunswick archæologists poke around in crumbling old walls and think that maybe perhaps who knows but what they might be walls that the Norsemen left. The proud knights of Spain came with war horses and their shining armor, but they did not succeed in implanting civilization until the women came. Daniel Boone forced his way down the dark rivers of Tennessee, but the wild tribesmen did not give up until the pioneer mothers followed with the washing and the churns. Then the Indians knew they were licked. The Apaches made short work of the strategists sent out from West Point, but the women of the lonely ranches of Arizona planted the white man's civilization and stuck.

Of all the heroes of our West, the most picturesque, the most gallant, chivalrous, and interesting was Juan Bautista de Anza. There was a good deal of bunk about Frémont, the famous pathfinder. One of the American pioneers said of him that he was 'The pathfinder who never found any paths; the conqueror who never won a battle, and the

CHURCH OF SAN MIGUEL HORCASITAS

millionaire without any money.' But De Anza was real and genuine.

In order to place him in the great drama of the West:

Francisco Vasquez Coronado, the young knight of Spain, discovered the West in 1540.

Father Kino made his explorations and his maps and his scientific deductions about one hundred and forty years later.

Ninety-seven years after Father Kino came Juan Bautista de Anza.

Captain de Anza was a young Spanish army officer stationed at a little presidio called Tubac. It lies north of Nogales on the highway between Nogales and Tucson. He was perhaps the first character of our country's history who could rightfully be called a Western man. He was born on the frontier of northern Mexico. His father had been an army officer before him.

Life must have been poison dull at the little garrison at Tubac... between Apache raids. The gay young captain's imagination called for action and adventure. There were, however, other reasons for his expedition. Important political reasons.

California had been discovered by a Portuguese sea captain named Cabrillo in 1542. He claimed the land for Spain — from which country he was getting his board and keep. Nothing was done of importance with the new land until two hundred years later. A long chain of churches was then established — the missions of California. On the part of the priests, this was a holy crusade to Christianize the heathen Indians. The Spanish Government had also another reason. Both Russia and England were nosing around California. If Spain hoped to hold the country, it was necessary to get people there.

After the establishment of the missions and the garrisons put there to protect them, great difficulty was experienced in providing them with food and other necessaries. It meant a long and difficult voyage from Mexico in tiny cockleshell ships — and the horrors of scurvy for the crews. Both the missions and the garrisons were always in dread of starvation.

Captain de Anza suggested to his superior officers that he thought he could find a way to cross the plains to California and open a land route to Mexico. Then they wouldn't have to bother or worry any more about the supply ships. He offered to pay the expenses of an exploring expedition to find out. After a great deal of red tape had been wound and unwound, he finally got permission and set out from Tubac on the 8th of January, 1774.

We will not spend much time with him on this first expedition. It was a brave and terrible journey. Out of his garrison of fifty soldiers at Tubac, he selected twenty seasoned veterans. As guides he had two brave priests who had made part of the journey alone — protected only by their faith. He carefully selected one hundred and forty tough little ponies and mules for the journey. Also sixty-five beef cattle to be killed for food *en route*. Just as he was getting ready to start, the Apaches swooped down from the hills and ran off his best animals. He had to make a détour back into Mexico and pick up what animals he could from the Father Kino missions. They were a poor lot.

Scorched by the desert heat, sometimes famished for want of water, lost in the dreaded sand hills of the Mojave; threatened and attacked by hostile Indians, De Anza

plodded over the terrible country which is still called
Camino de Diablo — road of the Devil. In a general way,
his route was through the modern town of Yuma; then
down into Mexico below the present town of Mexicali;
then north and through a pass of the mountains and finally
into the present city of Riverside. From there he made
his way north and arrived in Monterey on the 18th of
April, 1774.

Back at Tubac they had probably given him up for
lost, for there was no mail or news in that day. But just
as the sun was rising over the wild peaks of the Santa
Ritas on the morning of May 27, 1774, the sentry on watch
on the top of the Presidio walls saw long shadows moving
— gaunt and grotesque on the desert floor. He called the
corporal of the guard. They watched anxiously until the
far-off tiny figures appeared in the morning light; the
first rays of the sun caught and glittered on the steel of a
Spanish sword. It was De Anza's little army coming
home.

De Anza became famous almost overnight as the news
of his great adventure went from pueblo to pueblo —
all the way to the City of Mexico, where the great viceroy
lived in a palace. From captain he was promoted to
lieutenant-colonel. When he offered to make the trip to
California again, taking with him a company of settlers,
his offer was eagerly accepted. His offer was in fact a
life-saver for the Spanish Government. What with the
aggressions of Russia and England, the Spanish King
realized that it was of vital importance to plant a city on
the great harbor that we know now as San Francisco.
And he knew that no time was to be lost on the job.

There were no settlers at Tubac. Only a garrison of

soldiers. So De Anza sent word from one pueblo to another
telling the people that he intended to organize an expedition to cross the plains to the new land of California. He
told everyone who felt like going with him to come to the
little town of San Miguel Horcasitas. He selected that
place because at that time the governor of Sonora had
his capital there. De Anza stipulated that he would accept
no soldiers for the expedition except married men who
would bring their families along.

They came trooping in on horseback — on burros and
on foot — brave, adventurous men with dark-eyed wives
and children. Those must have been days of bustle and
confusion in that sleepy little adobe town — herds of
cattle bawling and rushing through the streets, vaqueros
yelling at them and flourishing their lassos, herds of pack-
horses driven in from the pasture lands, women and
children wandering around with their bundles, trying to
find a place to light, soldiers preparing their supplies,
muleteers rigging new straps on their pack-saddles, De
Anza himself giving orders from the porch of the Govern-
or's home.

At half-past four on the afternoon of September 29,
1775, the expedition finally trailed out from the town.
At the head of the column rode four mounted scouts,
watching every peak and cañon for signs of the dreaded
Apaches. They were all frontiersmen and veterans. Then
came De Anza with a few mounted soldiers. They carried
lances, swords, and guns. They wore armor made of
seven thicknesses of deerskin. Behind them came four or
five priests, heading a mingled company of men, women,
and children, riding on horses and mules, many of the
women with little children in their arms. Soldiers marched

on both sides of the column to guard the women and children. Some of these soldiers were volunteers selected by De Anza. From his garrison at Tubac he took eight soldiers, an officer, and a sergeant. With all the settlers and soldiers and priests and muleteers and herders there were two hundred and forty souls, of whom one hundred and sixty were women and children.

Behind the settlers came the herds of loose horses, mules, and horned cattle, stirring up clouds of dust, bawling and lowing. There were one hundred and twenty horses and twenty-five mules for the soldiers and their equipment; one hundred and twenty-five horses to carry the settlers and their baggage, three hundred and twenty head of beef cattle. For all these De Anza had to find food and water.

It was one of the most remarkable expeditions in human history. In latter days, engineers have builded roads along part of the route over which De Anza traveled, leading all these people. Digging for the roads, they often find mementoes of prehistoric tragedies, showing how terrible was the journey. They find broken water-bottles and bones, showing where some primitive traveler of a forgotten race had accidentally broken his olla and died of thirst — a slow terrible death in the sand hills. The young Spanish officer must have had a stout heart to lead this expedition.

De Anza did everything for the people he led. He rode with the scouts with every nerve strained as he watched for signs of the Indians. When evening came, he made the rounds to inquire after Mrs. Gomez's headache and asked Mrs. Lopez how her new baby's first tooth was getting on. Eight babies were born while the expedition was on the way. So tenderly did De Anza care for his charges during that frightful march that not one life was lost. One woman died just as they started, leaving her husband to march on alone with five little children. All the rest of the brave women endured heat and cold and thirst and dreadful dangers. They all arrived safely at Monterey at half-past ten on the morning of April 13, 1776.

De Anza saw them established in the new city of San Francisco which he founded. Then he started back to Mexico with a few soldiers. History tells how the settlers — particularly the women — followed him back along the road for a mile or more, their eyes streaming with tears, their broken voices asking God to bless and protect him.

In after years, these simple settlers who plodded through the desert wastes with De Anza became the proudest names in California. Many a lovely belle, with eyes sparkling from under her black lace mantilla and the little red heels of her satin shoes clicking through the fandango, remembered a grandmother who had carried a baby in her young arms as her mule plunged into the wild waters of the Colorado. And in many a proud California home — on an hacienda where the cattle fed on a thousand hills — hung a tattered coat of deerskin armor which Grandpa wore when he rode with De Anza.

We found the old town of San Miguel Horcasitas very much as it must have been in De Anza's day. The old stone church where he went to say his prayers on that last day is there just as he saw it, with its crude beams chipped by the axes of the Indian workmen; the old bells that rang a farewell to De Anza still ring to call the faithful to worship.

The day we were there, it was a Mexican holiday. The old adobe houses were gay with bunting. The lilt of Mexican music echoed through the sleepy old streets, just as though they were expecting De Anza to come riding into town.

CHAPTER IV

THE FIGHTING YAQUI

Two truckloads of armed soldiers rolled out of a side street in Guaymas and joined our expedition when we started through the Yaqui Indian country. I haven't as yet been able to figure out whether we should have swelled with the consciousness of having an escort of honor, or whether we should have broken out in gooseflesh pimples with premonitions of danger. Possibly both.

For you never can tell about a Yaqui. After four centuries of endless warfare, the Yaqui remains unconquered. Queen Elizabeth was on the throne of England when the proudest knights of Spain sallied out to conquer the Yaquis. The last army that went into the Yaqui country bent on conquest dropped bombs out of airplanes. But the throb-throb-throb of the Yaqui war-drums has never been stilled — except when the Yaqui got tired of thumping them.

It was two days since we had left Hermosillo. We had motored south to Guaymas. This is an old harbor town on the Gulf of California. Oddly enough it was once a way station on the trip between California and Arizona. Traveling over the old De Anza trail was an ordeal so frightful that the pioneers took a long way around. Freight and passengers for Arizona were embarked at San Francisco or San Pedro; shipped around Cape San Lucas into the Gulf of California to Guaymas; there they were transferred to a stern-wheel paddle steamer and run

up the Colorado River to Yuma. In this way they escaped
the desert sand hills, but usually spent a large part of
their time on the river sand bars. The river steamers
waded about as often as they swam.

Guaymas is a lovely old town: one of the loveliest in
Mexico. The mirror-like blue waters of the harbor reflect
the jagged peaks that surround the town. The first time
I saw Guaymas, the time was half an hour before daybreak. Strange unearthly figures slipped out of the fog
before us. It was as though the ghosts of the past were
scurrying back to their uneasy graves — a burro train
slipping along through the mist, old women with heavy
baskets on the way to the market, a squad of soldiers
passing on the way to relieve the guard, the sharp quick
orders of the sergeant coming to us out of the fog before
we could see the soldiers.

Guaymas should have plenty of ghosts to wander about
in the fog. There has been history. Great stately galleons
with painted sails used sometimes to take refuge there from
pirates. In the center of the town is a beautiful monument
erected to the memory of a battle in which the Mexican
women — peon women in black rebosos, aristocratic women in lace and fine linen — fought with guns by the side
of their husbands to repel the French who were trying to
capture the town.

It is one of the most famous fishing ports in the world.
Beautiful white ladylike yachts often lie in the harbor
while the millionaire sportsmen from the 'States' angle
for game fish. The warm waters of the Gulf are alive.
Enormous turtles float on the tropic waters.

We stopped at a charming old hotel with balconies
fully fifty feet wide looking down into a patio serene with

palms and flowers. A Mexican ship of war was anchored in the moonlit harbor and the sound of the ship's bell floated across the shimmering water to us as the hours were tolled. From this peaceful old place we went into the country of the Yaquis: we and our two truckloads of little bronzed soldiers. An ironic touch was added by a truckload of unarmed Yaquis sandwiched in between ourselves and our escorts. We could read this any way we liked. The Yaquis were doing us the high honor to escort us through their own country. But neither they nor we could avoid observing that if the other Yaquis were seized with an inspiration to start something, their own people would be a conspicuous part of the target.

Not that this would have worried the Yaquis very much. The Yaqui is one of the fiercest fighting men in the world. He is a little fellow with tiny hands and feet. He is usually as bashful as a little boy, but he has the heart of a fighting wildcat. When Yaqui mothers sing their babies to sleep, they have a lullaby, the refrain of which is: 'El Yaqui que sabe morir.' (The Yaqui who knows how to die.)

There have been three great fighting nations among the North American Indians. The Sioux with their allies the Cheyennes, the Apaches, and the Yaquis.

The Sioux made a great theatrical show of warfare. They galloped into battle wearing gorgeous war-bonnets of feathers; their ponies decorated on the shoulders with scarlet and blue patches of paint; pony tails wrapped with scarlet cloth. The warriors 'made up' for war with paint like chorus girls. Their battles were distinguished by dash and speed. They went into action with their ponies hitting the turf as fast as their little hoofs could pound. These battles were not so much a matter of killing the enemy as

of doing stunts. To win honors in battle, the warrior tried
to touch a foe with his hand or to whip him in the face with
his heavy quirt without killing him — at least before he
killed him. If a warrior could do this or could take away a
weapon from a living foe, he was awarded what was called
a 'coup stick,' which was a badge of high honor and gave
him the right to wear certain feathers in his hair. It was a
good deal like a college athlete getting a 'letter' for his
sweater. The white man's method of making war by whole-
sale slaughter rather horrified them. With them it was a
matter of glory and honor and daring — not of slaughter.

The Apache was, on the whole, a better fighter than the
Sioux, although the Sioux showed the highest type of military ability. The Apache, on the other hand, was a killer,
pure and simple. The Apaches taught their boys that a
warrior should be like a coyote: a sudden shot and a naked
figure slipping out of sight behind the rocks. It was matter of great shame to an Apache if one of the foe ever saw
him during a battle. His shots came out of nowhere.

During our twenty years war against the Apaches, our
soldiers seldom saw one, but there was not a minute that
the Apaches did not see the soldiers. A signal smoke curling
up in black spirals against the sky, a spit of flame, and a
soldier falls dying to the desert. Nothing to be seen but the
heat waves rising from the silent rocks. That was Apache
warfare. They didn't dress up like the Sioux. If the Apache
had human vanity, it did not take the form of feathers and
make-up. Like Kipling's Gunga Din, a bit of twisty rag
was all the field equipment he could find. A rag tied around
his head and a breech-clout with a pair of moccasins was
the Apache's war uniform.

The Yaqui had still a different method of making war.

Unlike the Sioux, he has usually been a foot soldier. He marches into battle to the beat of a Yaqui tom-tom: a little drum with a rawhide head. The pom-pom, pom-pom, pom-pom of this little drum freezes your blood: it seems so deadly and relentless. I have heard the Yaquis marching to the attack to the beat of this drum; and I don't want to hear it again.

As nearly as I can read the Yaqui's heart, he likes to fight in the same way that an American likes baseball. They seem to enjoy being shot at. In one of the recent Mexican revolutions, a large company of Yaquis were mobilized. They started on one side, and flopped over to the other side when the general changed his mind. It was all right with them. They didn't care on which side they fought.

One day I saw my little friend Pablo, the Yaqui, in the trenches at Naco. He was by this time on the Federal side, but he opened his coat and showed me that he was carrying the red badge of the rebels.

'Hey, Pablo,' I remonstrated, 'you are on the other side now.'

Pablo smiled a funny little smile and shrugged his shoulders. 'Well, one never knows,' he said.

When the revolution came unexpectedly to an end, Pablo and his Yaqui friends were outraged. They refused to go home. They said they had been invited to a fight and they wanted to fight somebody. They felt as though they had been invited to a party and sent home before the refreshments came.

In many ways the Yaqui isn't a bad sort of fellow. When he takes a job at some of the ranches, he is always a fine worker. His promises are solid gold. The worst you can say of him is there is considerable of the naughty boy in his make-up. He likes to swoop down on Mexican military posts just as a small boy likes to throw mud pies at passing automobiles.

I knew a young American sugar planter who, with his bride, was taken captive by a band of Yaqui raiders. They held him a prisoner for two or three weeks and he said he had a wonderful time. They let him go on the war trail with them; even let him beat the tom-tom. He said, when they started out on the war-trail, the Yaqui women and girls shouted and cheered exactly as the co-eds cheer for the players at a football game. He said that most of the expeditions he saw were forays against Mexican travelers. The Yaquis thought it a great joke to take all their clothes and let them go. There was nothing vicious or cruel about their little games of war-making. Sometimes, it must be confessed, that his enthusiasm has led the Yaqui into horrible atrocities.

You can also say this for the Yaqui. His wars were forced upon him. Away back in the early days of Mexico — three or four hundred years ago — the Spaniards took all the loot they could find in the great Aztec empire to the south. Then they wanted more. They had an idea that the Aztecs had wonderful mines on the West Coast and sent armies up to drive out the Indians. The driving was pretty good until they got to the Yaquis. You must remember that these Spanish troops were the finest soldiers in Europe, trained under great captains and war-hardened by terrific campaigns against the Aztecs. The Yaquis gave them a terrible licking and beat every army sent against them for the next four centuries. Since Mexico became a republic its armies have been almost continuously at war with the Yaquis.

It hasn't been all beer and skittles for the Yaqui. Time after time the Yaquis have been all but annihilated. I have read of campaigns in which they were so ragged and frozen that at night they buried themselves in the earth up to the neck, to crawl out and fight again the next day. Badly beaten in one war, a shipload of Yaquis were loaded for exile. They threw their women and children overboard and leaped into the sea themselves, preferring death to separation from their wild mountains.

At last a very shrewd President of Mexico made a treaty with them whereby every Yaqui warrior received thirty dollars a month just to be good. Since then the Yaquis have behaved pretty well. But when the harvest moon comes up over the mysterious mountains, the little Yaqui begins to get queer feelings. His heart grows uneasy and he thinks how sweet a song the bullet sings as it whines past his ears, or cracks from the muzzle of his own rifle. Then he is likely to slip away from his neat little towns by the side of the railroad where the Mexican Government tells him to live. They miss his face at roll-call and little fires twinkle in the dim silent cañons of his mysterious mountains and nobody has any desire to go in and try to bring him out.

In the end he will be conquered; but by schoolbooks rather than bullets. The Mexican Government has opened schoolhouses in the Yaqui country. And the Yaqui children, who are as smart as little fox terriers, are forgetting the song about the Yaqui who knows how to die.

Nevertheless, one can never be too sure about a Yaqui. We didn't feel too sure as we rode along highways bordered by thick chaparral. It did not cheer us a great deal to see the Mexican road-builders working with picks and shovels in their hands, loaded rifles on their backs, and revolvers dangling from their hips.

I imagine that in the days of the Roman Empire, when the legions of the great Julius Cæsar were guarding the river Rhine against the barbarians who came out of the dark forests, their forts must have looked just like the Yaqui country. For about a hundred miles we traveled through a desert lined with forts. These forts are of mud with a little tower on top of each one. Under an awning or thatched brush, to shield him from the blazing sun, a sentry stands all day, his rifle in his hands and his eyes always anxiously scanning the horizon; his ears always listening for the tom-tom, tom-tom — the Yaqui drums.

On one side of the railroad track are five or six neat clean little towns, villages for the Yaquis built by the Mexican Government. On the other side of the tracks are the forts and the Mexican soldiers. To prevent the Yaquis stealing up for a secret attack, the brush has been cleared off for a long distance around each adobe fort. In some places the Yaqui boys have used the cleared places for basket-ball courts. Which is what I should call sarcasm.

We didn't hear the beat of the Yaqui war drums. In fact, the Yaquis seemed to think the sight of us under heavy guard was rather funny. They hung their heads and made little snickering remarks to each other as they stood around in groups in the Mexican garrison towns. They looked as though they wanted to say: 'A lot of good all those soldiers would do you if we took a notion.'

We drove a long way through the Yaqui country until, at last, we came to the famous Yaqui River.

There is a saying in Mexico: 'Once you have drunk the waters of the Yaqui River, you will always return.' And I am not sure that this is not true. This mysterious river is a sullen, muddy stream that winds and turns through a flat country, willow trees clinging to the banks. The Yaquis — just to show their friendly feelings and also to earn a few pesos — helped our motor cars to cross the river on their ferry. No one knows how many years they have been running it. Their ferryboat is a flat scow called a pango. It is managed by half a dozen Yaquis with long oars. The current is very swift, so they row upstream as far as they can and let the pango drift down to the opposite bank. Sometimes when the pango does not behave very well, two or three Yaquis jump overboard into the rushing stream and haul the boat by main strength to the bank. One of our cars broke through the deck of the pango and it took a whole company of Mexican soldiers to lift it out.

Climbing the opposite bank of the river Yaqui, we found ourselves in a different kind of country. It was as though we had suddenly come through a curtain into a new world.

CHAPTER V

WE FIND A PLAYMATE

His name, he said, was Nicolas Pinto, but he asked me as a special favor to call him El Norteño (The Northerner). It made him feel more adventurous; although it seemed to me that he was having plenty of adventures without the assistance of a new name. We couldn't find any such word as 'Norteño' in the Spanish dictionary, so I imagine that Nicolas must have made it up. However, most of the adventurers of the world have made their own names, so we will have to ignore the Spanish purists and let his stand as he made it.

Nicolas was a little Mexican boy we picked up on a lonely road in the Mayo Indian country. He wasn't so little at that, being tall for his age and as straight as a ramrod. He was sixteen years old. When we first saw him, he was wearing everything he owned in the world — which consisted of a pair of ragged white cotton trousers, a 'hickory' shirt, and an enormous sombrero. His bare feet were thrust into a pair of rawhide guarachas — just two pieces of cowhide with straps to hold them on.

El Norteño was trying to walk from the south of Mexico to the United States. He lived in a lonely little town in the mountains back of the city of Guadalajara. For a year he had worked at odd jobs to save money enough to come to California of which he had heard so much. He went without candy and stayed home from the circus and hoarded every centavo.

Guadalajara was the first big city he had ever seen. He fell in there with a man who said he was going to the United States. El Norteño was delighted with the man's suggestion that they should travel together. He thought it was a fine idea when the man offered to take care of all of his saved-up money so it would not get lost. One day they started down to the railroad to begin the grand journey. At the last moment the man sent El Norteño on an errand around the corner. When the boy hurried back, his friend was gone. Also El Norteño's money. He never saw either again.

El Norteño dried his tears and started to walk two thousand miles to the promised land.

The Mexican peon is very kind and generous. If he has only one tortilla, he will insist that you take the bigger half of it. These simple-hearted country people felt sorry for the boy and helped him on his way from one pueblo to the next. Nevertheless, El Norteño was a very tired and very hungry boy when we picked him up on the road. He was so delighted at being adopted by los americanos that he forgot all about going to the United States. He turned back south with us. All the rest of the way through Mexico, El Norteño was one of our party. We all grew so fond of him that we made up our minds to bring him back to the United States. You shall see before this book is finished whether we did or not.

I have met many men in many lands, but it has never been my lot to know a finer, truer gentleman than this little Mexican peasant boy. He was very poor, but the blood of an ancient chivalry must have run in El Norteño's veins. He had the pride of an aristocrat.

One day he had done something so brave and so unselfish

that we all wanted to do something for him. One of the engineers collected a purse of nine dollars which — changed into Mexican pesos — filled a sack. This he put into El Norteño's lap as he lay asleep in one of the automobiles. At daylight the next morning, there came a tap at the door of the leader of the party. It was El Norteño. In silence he handed back the money and walked away, leaving us very much ashamed at having done something so raw and tactless. He was a little cool toward us all that day.

When I got up in the morning, I always found El Norteño in the lobby of the hotel. In Spanish he would ask if I had slept well. If I said that I had, he always replied with grave dignity, 'I thank God that he has bestowed upon you the blessing of sleep." The only English he knew were two words, 'Fine' and 'pencil' — which he called 'pin-ceel.' Sometimes when it was very hot and the dust was choking me and I felt in a mood for a murder, El Norteño would come to the door of the automobile and say: 'Fine?' He really said 'Fi-en.' And I would just have to answer 'Fine.' No grouch could resist that grin.

At night he slept in one of the automobiles or on the ground wrapped up in an old ragged blanket. No matter how cold the night or how blistering the day, El Norteño never uttered a word of complaint. He was game to the backbone. The boy became an ever-present help. No one could pick up anything or carry anything. All the rest of the trip through Mexico, Norteño's shapely brown hands were always carrying our bundles and picking up what we had dropped. He helped in more ways than politeness. We should never have understood Mexico so well without him.

As we climbed up the south bank of the Rio Yaqui, we

found the band from a cavalry regiment waiting to welcome us into a country different from anything else we had seen in Mexico. It fascinated El Norteño, although it was old stuff to us. Big gasoline tractors, irrigating ditches and cotton gins — fields of wheat and rice. It was like a big American farm dropped into the middle of Mexico. The northern part of Mexico, along the border, is much like Arizona — great stretches of vacant land — unused for want of water — cattle-ranges, high, rugged mountains, gashed with mining tunnels.

The Rio Yaqui, which for so many centuries was a deadly barrier beyond which civilization might not go, has finally been the means of bringing progress to Mexico. Some years ago, American engineers imprisoned the wild waters of the Yaqui and turned them into irrigation ditches to water great tracts of farmland. These lands are in the hands of progressive American business men and progressive Mexicans. Foremost among these Mexicans was former President Obregon.

The entire lay-out of farms, irrigation ditches, and so on is called the 'Yaqui Project.' More than a hundred and twenty-five thousand acres have been planted in wheat, rice, henequén, and early vegetables — tomatoes, lettuce, and so on. More than eight hundred miles of irrigation ditches criss-cross the place, bringing in water enough to flood the million acres they expect to plant.

When we looked at this vast modern farm project, we realized what Mexico will be like some day. The peaceful picturesque old adobes will give place to hideous warehouses of concrete and galvanized iron. The patient oxen that we saw plowing with crooked sticks will be driven away by the snort and grunt of the gasoline tractor. It will not be long until the peon gives up his white cotton pants and guarachas and blossoms out in copper-riveted overalls and shoes. Mexico will not be the beautiful, peaceful land of mañana very long.

El Norteño did not share our melancholy regret that Mexico must emerge some day from its sleepy picturesqueness and become a noisy, slam-bang, hurry-up, step-on-it-kid land like all the rest of the world. El Norteño held out a welcoming hand to progress. We almost had to throw him down and sit on him to keep him from trying to run the biggest tractor in the 'Yaqui Project.' Its snort and grunt made sweet music in his ears.

Long ago, when Montezuma, the great Aztec king, ruled Mexico, he liked fish for breakfast. There being no fish in the lakes near the City of Mexico that pleased him, his breakfast had to be brought to him by runners.

At sunset every night a solemn official handed a fresh fish to a naked runner at the seaport of Vera Cruz. The runner grabbed the fish and lit out like a scared jack-rabbit. He ran as fast as he could to another Indian runner and handed him the fish. This runner ran to a third naked man, standing all poised for a fast start. Hundreds of runners kept up a relay race all night at top speed — two hundred and sixty-five miles over mountains and through deep cañons. At breakfast, the fish was always there for the king.

I thought of that old relay race when I saw the fast freights standing on the sidings at Ciudad Obregon, with steam up, ready to start, with a scream of whistles, on the long trip over mountains and rivers and plains to Chicago and New York, rushing lettuce and tomatoes and other fresh vegetables so that the people at the big hotels could have what they wanted for breakfast when their own farms lay deep under the snow. The mighty dramas of the world — the wars, the explorations, the march of progress — have mostly been connected with the job of getting food from one place to another. I shall have to confess that this is an entirely unworthy thought for so big a subject; but I never think of those silent Indian runners panting through the night that I do not think how awful it would have been if — after all that relay race — the king's cook had burned the fish!

There are two important towns in the Yaqui Project. One was formerly called Cajeme — after a famous Yaqui chief. When President Obregon was murdered, just as he retired from office, the name was changed to Ciudad Obregon (See-oo-dad Obregon), which means City of Obregon. The other town is called Navojoa (Navo-hoh-a).

Night had fallen when we left Ciudad Obregon to go to Navojoa, where we were to sleep. We ran the cars, one at a time, on the pango ferryboats which carried us across the Rio Mayo — the Mayo River. It was dark night and the headlights of the cars threw weird grotesque shadows on the half-naked figures of the Mayo Indians up to their necks in the swift-flowing river, struggling to tug the pangos against the current. This river divides the ancient land of the Mayos from the country of the Yaquis.

The Mayos are a people as mysterious as the Yaquis. They are the only blue-eyed Indians I have ever seen. Many scientists believe they are descendants of the ancient Aztecs over whom the fish-eating emperor Montezuma ruled and who were conquered by the Spanish knights in the savage battles of the Conquest. They themselves say that they are related to the Yaquis — sort of cousins; but scientists do not agree as to this. Many think that the Yaquis are related to the Apaches and to the Navajos, a fierce, independent tribe of northern Arizona who make the blankets and the silver jewelry we all know so well. Other scientists think that the Yaquis are related to the Pima Indians of southern Arizona and that the Mayos are no relation.

I once asked one of my Apache friends about this. He gave a very haughty reply. 'Well,' he said, 'the Yaqui is kind of mixed. He is partly Apache, partly Spanish, and partly of the blood of the Negro slaves who were brought over by the Spanish from Africa.' He puffed at his cigarette and added: 'The Apache part is good.'

The Mayo isn't as full of fight as the Yaqui; at least he doesn't regard fighting as his favorite form of outdoor sport. But he can fight bravely and terribly. In the last Mexican revolution, I saw a band of Mayos charging a trench — walking into a storm of bullets — with gay indifference as though it were a lovely party. One of the Mayos was shot (a great many were shot, but I remember this one especially). As the order came for them to retreat, the friend and buddy of this wounded Mayo would not leave him. Under heavy fire he dragged his wounded friend into a little cemetery where the tombstones were pink and blue with funny little angels carved in stone. All day long he lay behind a pink tombstone, with his body sheltering the body of his friend. They poured bullets from fourteen machine guns down upon him. The air fairly buzzed and whined with bullets, but he seemed to bear a charmed life. Every time a hand or a head showed above the top of the trench, one of his bullets spat out death. When night came and darkness fell, he picked up his friend, flung him to his shoulder like a sack of grain, and staggered out into the night. As a final farewell, his voice came out of the dark with the worst insult you can possibly offer a Mexican, 'Adios, you old goats!' he yelled to the soldiers who had been shooting at him.

The Mayos are famous for making blankets. They are very beautiful, being artistic mixtures of blue and green and brown. They are not as stiff and unwieldy as the Navajo blankets. The Navajos weave theirs of sheep's wool; the Mayos use goat's hair. Many of the Mayos work on the great farms of the Yaqui Project and are good, faithful workers. At certain times of the year, however, they leave the tractors and slip out into secret places in the mountains, where they have strange heathen ceremonies — ceremonies which have come down to them from a mysterious and distant past.

They have a strange legend about their river. They still believe the story about the Seven Golden Cities of Cibola for which Coronado the explorer was searching. They believe it is somewhere up in the mountains at the headwaters of the Rio Mayo. They think it has been there for untold ages and that the inhabitants are a very wise, almost godlike people. When the spring rains come and the waters of the Rio Mayo tear down in wild floods, they find floating boards carved with outlandish inscriptions. The Mayos believe that these markings on the boards are in the language of a forgotten and mysterious people who are trying to send them messages on the flood waters of the river.

The Mayos have great ideas of loyalty. In the last Mexican revolution a band of Indians — both Yaquis and Mayos — joined the rebel side. Their commander was a

big handsome Mayo Indian whose name was General
Yucopicio. When the revolution ended and the other
soldiers went home to their farms, General Yucopicio did
not take his Indians home. They vanished one night and
were next heard of in the wild fastnesses of the mountains.
One day, months afterward, they came trailing out of the
mountains into Navojoa. The Mexicans asked General
Yucopicio why he had done this thing. He refused to tell
them. 'I report only to my chief,' he said with dignity.
Whereupon he went all alone to the grave of President
Obregon, who had been his friend and commander, and
told him the secret of the Indian soldiers who would not go
home.

We stopped at a very quaint old Mexican hotel in
Navojoa. The bellboys and porters were all Mayo
Indians. At night they slept out on the stone steps of the
hotel. They didn't really lie down, but simply propped
themselves up against the door and snoozed off — wrapped
in their lovely Mayo blankets. This made it difficult to get
through the door. You had to step *on* them or step *over*
them. Having seen the Mayos fighting, I thought it best
not to step *on* them. Who knows but that one of them
might have been the little fellow who fought all that day
against the fire of fourteen machine guns in the cemetery at
Naco!

CHAPTER VI

THE GRINGO INVASION

THE rich agricultural country between the Rio Yaqui and the old Aztec city of Culiacan has begun to sprout Yankees. All through this country you find the Mexican burro stepping aside to let an American tractor pass. And then he ambles along at his own pace, refusing to be stampeded from the seventeenth century into the twentieth.

In the lovely valley of the Rio Fuerte — just across the state line between Sinaloa and Sonora — is an old town called Los Mochis which has 'gone American.' It is in the heart of the sugar-cane country. All the land, the sugar-mills, the hotel, and most of the business firms are owned by Americans. The plantations are operated with modern American efficiency. The planters live a life that reminds one of Rudyard Kipling's stories of the life of the English in India. They have their tennis clubs, polo fields, golf links, dances, bridge parties. It is as though they lived on a gay island in a sad and changeless ocean called Mexico. And, as usual in such communities, what they know about each other's private affairs is plenty. It is interesting to see how these outlanders have fitted themselves into Mexico. The grand mansion of Los Mochis is half English, half rural Spanish — set in a lovely English garden.

Some of the most charming homes I have ever seen have been made by American girls in Mexico. They have spread a lovely veneer of Yankee over old houses, mostly in the way of plumbing and comfortable chairs.

Mexican houses lack comfort. The old ones have heavy elegance and no conveniences. The new ones are long on loggias, potted palms, and stiff furniture.

The worst are the newly rich Mexicans who have 'gone Hollywood.'

Right in the middle of the American town is a part of Los Mochis where the Mexican laborers live with their families — just as their people have lived for centuries — same old sandals, white cotton drawers, sombreros, and tortillas. The one feature of American civilization for which the Mexicans seem to have reached with eagerness is American jazz dance music. I have never seen a Mexican town so small that it did not have an orchestra. I never found an orchestra that did not play 'Show Me the Way to Go Home' — just then the popular favorite. Perhaps, however, this doesn't mean so much after all. Jazz music is so primitive that it still smells of the African jungles.

In this spatter-work country — half American and half seventeenth-century Mexico — it was interesting to see how the two races get along. On principle the Mexican peon feels that he ought to hate the Gringo invader; but he never can find any particular one that he doesn't like. Nearly every Mexican likes to work for an American boss. The majority of Americans who go down into this district are clever, sympathetic, likable college boys.

A very curious fact seems to be that four fifths of the Mexican women of the better class yearn to move to Hollywood; but the American women like to live in Mexico. An American girl who goes to Mexico to establish a home finds herself a grand lady of the Middle Ages with swarms of gentle, amiable servants. This is an old story to the Mexican girl, who has been brought up that way. She

wants to move to Hollywood; dine in cafés at the next
table to Mary Pickford.

Account for this as you will, but my observation is that
the average Mexican man is sinking deeper into Mexico all
the time — burrowing in with a fierce and mysterious devotion. The peons of Indian blood are breeding back to the
mother race. Among the intellectual classes the men are
reaching down into Mexico's heritage of spiritual mystery
and strength — a heritage left by old races and forgotten
civilizations. On the other hand, the Mexican woman — as
though fearful of lifting the lid of that ancient Pandora's
box — is usually found with her face turned toward Hollywood. This may be because Los Angeles is essentially a
woman's town in every characteristic. It is the capital
city of the She World.

It follows that any account of this section of Mexico
must be a spatter-work — a good deal like the country itself — random notes of a traveler.

'Gun-packing' is as common in rural Mexico as in the
old days of our border. But not for the same reason. A
gunfight is almost unheard of — I think it is a left-over
from the days of chivalry. They wear guns in the same
way that the Spanish knights wore swords. I asked one
charming young engineer on the staff of the Governor of
Sinaloa why he went about draped with artillery. He
laughed and answered, 'Es mi joya.' (It is my jewel.)

To a Mexican, it is incomprehensible that in our big
cities we allow ourselves tamely to be held up by thugs in
the street. One of the two would come home dead in
Mexico. Mexican ladies tell me that, during the early days
before the bandits were cleaned up, they always expected

to see a revolver laid on the seat of the limousine when they went out in the evening.

I embarrassed the distinguished mayor of the little town of Elota very much by feeling the outlines of the six-gun under his coat. He came back to me, with three different interpreters in relays, to make it clear that he wasn't a bad man; that the revolver was his insignia of office; and that, anyhow, he was only carrying it in order that he might have the privilege of laying down his life in my defense.

It is said jocosely that you can detect a Mexican's social rank by his revolver holster. Possibly there are so many beautiful holsters because Mexico has so many generals. Whatever the explanation may be, it remains a fact that some of the finest examples of native arts and crafts are to be found on pistol scabbards. The leather is beautifully carved and sometimes handsomely embroidered in gold and silver thread. Usually they are worn dangling from belts filled with cartridges that have been polished until they gleam. I have even known Mexican dandies who had their cartridges made of solid silver. They couldn't be fired, of course, silver being too soft a metal; but they provided grand ornamentation.

Near the busiest part of this section of Mexico is a 'ghost town.' An old port on the Gulf which once was famous for turtles. It has an Indian name — Agiabampo. When the Americans built a railroad down the West Coast, some years ago, they laid the tracks many miles east of Agiabampo. They left it marooned. Now it is slumbering in its memories — falling into decay — leaning walls and falling timbers. The smothering growth of the banyan trees is creeping up upon it. The old well-sweep seemed to whisper little echoes of the laughter of the peon women... crumbling walls of adobe houses...

If the glory has gone, the turtles have not. Thousands of them float in the warm tropic waters — enormous fellows weighing two or three hundred pounds. These Mexican Gulf waters are the greatest turtle hunting-grounds in the world. There are times when the sea seems paved with tortoise-shells.

Sea turtles are clumsy old fellows with heads that look fierce — but are not. Their necks look like the necks of old, old men that have been washed and shrunken in the process. They have no teeth — merely a hard jaw made for snapping off seaweed, upon which they feed. It is this diet that sometimes gives their flesh a tinge of green. Native turtle fishers say they have caught giants weighing a thousand pounds, but I have never seen one that weighed more than three hundred to five hundred. No one knows to what age they live: probably one hundred to three hundred years.

There are two common ways of catching the turtles. The natives dive from boats and grab them by the flippers, dragging them in over the gunwales of the boats. The simplest way is to wait until the females come ashore to lay their eggs, then turn them over on their backs. They have no fight in their souls. They peer out with a sort of pained contemplation and walk with a heavy deliberation of manner that suggests an undertaker walking on a hot plate and trying not to lose his professional manner. They don't indulge in much conversation in their three hundred years. At egg-laying time, the females have a sort of tame hiss like that of an indolent snake. The males have a species of weak bellow at the mating season which the young lady turtles of a mere fifty or sixty years no doubt find alluring and romantic.

The books contend that the turtles cannot live very long on land because the bottom of their shell houses is soft and cannot properly hold up their gizzards without the support of the sea water. However, I knew a family at Riverside, California, who kept one as a pet for fifteen years and he died — amidst the mourning of an afflicted family — with gizzard still intact. He was an affectionate old chap and would follow the family all over the garden.

In the days before fishing boats had mechanical refrigeration, the crews often used to take whole deckloads of turtles on board — they turned them over on their backs and used them as needed for food. The turtles never seemed to suffer from these protracted periods of meditation with their feet in the air.

We visited many great estates — kingdoms of the soil; but at Agiabampo, we had luncheon at a little country farm — the Mexican version of one of our Iowa farms. The farmhouse was a one-story adobe, built flush to the road — iron-barred windows and a great door leading through the house to the patio. On the porch that fronted this patio, the life of the family was lived. Wooden pegs were at one end of the porch. Upon them straddled the saddles of the men of the family. Nearly every saddle carried a sword — the Mexican machete. The patio was not a flower garden as in the more elegant Mexican houses. This was a farmyard, with turtle meat drying in strips and shreds, the skins of wild animals, coyotes and foxes, drying on a rawhide clothesline.

At this old ranch we had a chance to see a real farm

kitchen. It was in a little square adobe house in the courtyard, away from the house. The stove was made of stone
and adobe bricks. Under each separate stove-hole was a
separate fire. If cooking three things, you have three fires.
Usually these fires are made by charcoal, of which Mexico
produces enormous quantities. As a usual thing, when an
American girl goes to Mexico to live, she gives one scornful
look at the Mexican stove and sends to the 'States' for a
shiny cook-stove. In the end the shiny cook-stove makes a
grand table upon which to pile the dishes. The American
girl invariably goes back to the Mexican stove.

The little town of Guasave was so sleepy that it looked as
though it had not stirred for three hundred years. But it
was stirred this time. The village band in white cotton
drawers and sandals was tooting its head off in our honor.
Peons in big sombreros milled and surged around our cars,
very anxious to see los americanos. A gentleman, with
heavy silver embroidery on his sombrero and an enormous
revolver hanging from his belt, scattered them and led us,
as he explained with great dignity, to the 'Municipal
Palace.'

The 'Municipal Palace' turned out to be a little adobe
house with a big front room. This room was adorned with
crayon portraits of the heroes of Mexico. With handsome
impartiality, the mayor had hung the portraits of the
presidents and the chiefs who had risen in revolution
against the presidents; and the revolutionists who had
risen against the revolutionists.

We all made speeches. Every time any of us rose to
speak, the village band played a thrilling little flourish
which is called 'The Diana.' I was overcome with self-

importance until I found out that they always play 'The
Diana' at bull-fights to celebrate the moment when the
bull comes in. After that I wasn't so sure that I ought to
feel complimented.

After the speeches, we went out onto the long porch that
looked out into the patio. At one end of this porch was a
dark adobe room with a barred door. It was the town jail.
It had one occupant. He was the most forlorn-looking indi-
vidual I ever remember to have seen. His cotton pants
were torn; his sombrero was banged in on one side, and he
had lost one of his guarachas. To the obvious displeasure
of the Mexican grandees, we passed cigars and cigarettes
and money to him through the bars. One of us, with a
grand inspiration, passed him a stick of tutti-frutti chew-
ing-gum. El Nortoño, to whom gum was a new and pride-
ful accomplishment, showed him how to chew it. He
chewed it without any enthusiasm. Mournful and uncon-
vinced, he cast a dejected eye upon El Norteño as that
young caballero showed him how to bubble. This is one of
the more delicate and intricate advances in the art of gum-
chewing. But he refused even to try to bubble. He sank
down to the floor on his heels and sadly began chewing his
cud as though gum-chewing were one more ill and sorrow
that a cruel fate had thrust upon him.

Afterward we went out to a grove of enormous banyan
trees, where they were getting ready a turtle barbecue in
our honor. One elderly peon was the barbecue champion
of the place. He dug a pit in the ground and built a fire
while two or three assistants, with bowie knives which they
unlimbered from their belts, shred the turtle meat into
flaky fragments. They finally had a great pottery bowl

brimming over. When it was finally cooked, they put it on
a long table which fairly sagged with the weight of tortillas,
chicken, and enchiladas. I wasn't so crazy about the turtle
meat. It seemed rather flat and tasteless.

One lone American had lived in the town for more than
twenty years. He was a doctor who had graduated from a
famous university. A great sorrow had come into his life.
He had come to Mexico to get away from the scenes of his
grief. For all these years he had lived in a strange land,
caring for the sick and poor. He seemed very poor himself,
for his clothes were shabby and threadbare. But he was
gentle and kind. He said he had found happiness among
these simple and kindly people who so greatly needed his
help.

If we made a stir in the life of Guasave, we fairly stood
Guamuchil on its head with excitement. There is one little
country inn at Guamuchil. I suppose that, on its big
nights, it had two guests. You can imagine then the excitement of the innkeeper when he saw our party with our
cavalcade of cars coming in one direction and the Governor
of the great State of Sinaloa coming in the other direction
with his whole staff — snappy West-Point-looking young
men in natty uniforms. He came as near dashing around as
a Mexican has ever been known to dash. All the regular
parlor boarders were sent flying out in all directions to find
beds wherever they could.

A long table was spread down the middle of the patio. A
Mexican Paul Revere was sent galloping from ranch to
ranch to pick up the members of the village orchestra.
They left their plows and hoes and came hurrying in with
their instruments. Dressed in shirt-sleeves and white

cotton pants, they played most of the night for us. Out of special compliment, they tried to play American jazz music until we sent a message asking them for Mexican tunes. These Mexican folk-songs are charming. No one knows who composed most of them. They were made up by the herders, riding around the cattle at night; by little peons as they followed the burro trains down lonely trails. One song very popular in Mexico is *Cuatro Milpas*. It is a very sad song. It tells of a farmer who came back from fighting in a revolution to find his little farm in ruins — his four fields a wreck. The name of the song means 'Four Fields.'

These folk-songs well up from the soil. They are the nearest that America has ever come to a native music. Jazz is more Jewish than Negro. Negro spirituals echo from Africa. What we call Spanish music — like *La Paloma* — is of the music halls — composed songs. The real songs of Mexico just happened. The Mexicans are a very lovable and warm-hearted people. They are happy when they can make you happy. The peon musicians, in from the fields with their time-stained guitars and their shabby fiddles, were happy when we applauded and demanded 'Mas! Mas!' which means 'More! more!'

I had a room with a bed that had been made by native workmen. Instead of springs it had rawhide thongs crisscrossed underneath. The room looked out through an iron-barred window onto the sidewalk. It had no curtains. When I went to bed that night, I had an interested audience. It seemed as though about half the town crowded around the window — dark, silent faces under big sombreros. They watched me pull off my heavy field boots and crawl in under the gay Mayo blanket.

The Governor looked a little tired and worn the next morning. Finding there weren't enough to go around, he had insisted that the Gringos have all the beds. He had slept on a billiard table. Which I call the final height of hospitality.

CHAPTER VII

THE HACIENDA COUNTRY

NICOLAS snickered when he heard some of our party talking about haciendas. This is one word that, with great gusto, has been ushered into the English language.

Hacienda! Realtors announce haciendas with tiled bathrooms and breakfast nooks. Which El Norteño thought was very funny.

An hacienda is not a house. It is an estate, more especially a great farm which is in active operation. It must be working to be an hacienda. El Norteño even protested when we called cattle-ranges haciendas. The meaning of the word implies activity — doing — working... A rancho has come to mean a farm of two thousand acres or under. More land than that becomes an hacienda.

Until you have seen the Mexican haciendas you have not seen Mexico. We came into the hacienda country as we crossed the line from Sonora into Sinaloa, just south of the old turtle town, Agiabampo. It was like slipping back into the Middle Ages. The hacendados — as the owners of haciendas are called — rule like ancient barons in their castles. In fact, the titles of these great estates run back, in many instances, to the Spanish Conquest. Life flows on much as it did four hundred years ago.

I am going to tell you about two or three haciendas that we visited. I select these because they are typical and characteristic.

One was called Los Pericos, which El Norteño told us

are delicious, but some are so hot that you feel like calling out the fire department with every bite. After witnessing with some awe the stuff that Norteño could swallow, I decided he must be lined inside with asbestos.

Norteño opened an iron door in the kitchen wall and we found that it opened into a Mexican oven that stood in the back courtyard. It was made of adobe brick and looked like an old-fashioned beehive. The Mexican housewife puts wood into the oven; burns it until the bricks are almost red-hot; then she rakes it out and puts in the bread or whatever she wishes to cook. American women who have used them tell me that these ovens are better than modern stoves.

The courtyard in which the oven stood was really a fort. It was built for military defense. The gates were of heavy, studded timbers. In time of danger they drove the stock and the families inside and shut the gates against attack. All around the edges of the courtyard were small rooms of adobe. Some were used as quarters for the servants; others were workshops where the peons made leather harness, bridles for the horses, reatas, and so on.

At dinner I told the señora that I wished I could live in such a lovely old place where everything was so peaceful and quiet. 'Well,' she said, 'if you had to manage all these servants for a while, you wouldn't like it so well.' She told me she would like to live in Hollywood. She became quite excited when she told me about a Hollywood bungalow she had seen — where you just touch a button and it gets light; another, and it gets dark; another button, and the room gets warm; another, and it gets cold.

El Norteño was politely skeptical. He didn't believe in magic.

A GATE IN THE HACIENDA COUNTRY

We had luncheon in a long dining-room at the end of a porch; it was furnished with ancient black walnut furniture, huge highboys and a marvelous old carved table. One of the guests at the luncheon was a dentist who travels from hacienda to hacienda with his dental chair packed in a specially made automobile. He was an American. If you have a toothache on a Mexican hacienda, there is nothing to do but grin and bear it until the 'tooth doctor' comes motoring along.

This dentist, who was a charming fellow, told me a good deal about the tusks of Mexico. He said that the Mexican peasant looks as though he had perfect teeth, but this is not always true. The reason the teeth appear so white and so perfect is the background of his dark skin. The peasants suffer a great deal from indigestion and this disease reflects itself in their teeth. The fiery chile that they eat chews up the linings of their stomachs and the mescal and tequila that they drink stops the action of their gastric juices. The dentist formerly had an office in one of the Mexican cities, but left it to become a tramp dentist because he likes to wander around among the country peons. They are a charming and appealing people. To my not inconsiderable surprise, he told me that, even as a town dentist, he found the peons were always good pay. A Mexican family will go without eating to pay the dentist or the doctor.

The infant mortality among the peons is dreadful. The children of the poor fade away like little flowers. It is perhaps a reflection upon the sorrow and hardships of the cruel life of the peon that the death of a child is always made the occasion of at least pretended rejoicing — the little soul that is admitted to heaven without having to endure the sufferings of life.

A week later, I visited another hacienda, La Puga, so regal in its proportions and its manner of life that it made Los Pericos seem a little country farm. La Puga has belonged to the Aguirre family since the days of the Conquest. It has a Spanish coat-of-arms set into the patio wall which shows the fortification was built in 1683. There is so much land in this estate that it baffles the imagination — more than five million acres. Mountain ranges, river valleys, lush meadow-lands.

The long cool balcony of the ranch-house looks out upon the burned-out craters of Sanguanguey and the blue peaks of the Santiagos. Stone steps go down from this balcony onto the cobble-stoned road leading to the corrals. Always onto this road the master of the hacienda looks down upon a restless stream of activity — the life of the rancho: long six-span ox-teams plodding into the compounds dragging huge two-wheel carts loaded mountain-high with sugar-cane or hemp fiber; vaqueros driving herds of cow-ponies, steers that break into sudden panics and try to escape down side roads while the vaqueros flourish their reatas and yell; long pack-trains of burros loaded with cane and hay — the daily life of a working farm.

From the inner balcony of the house one looks down into the patio where the intimate family life of the household goes on; quiet servant-women in rebosos pattering along on errands of the house; women patting tortillas at the enormous ovens; laundry-women patting the linen at the stone tubs which are really like overgrown horse-troughs.

It seems as though you had slipped back into the Middle Ages when you go down to the first floor under the balcony and see the men-at-arms on guard. Since the days of its founding, La Puga has maintained a garrison of soldiers.

The first soldiers who loitered around that porch were Spanish soldiers in deerskin armor with bell-muzzled arquebuses. The soldiers who loaf around there now have modern Mauser rifles leaning against the walls. Just back of the barracks-room is a dining-room for the soldiers. How many rollicking songs have been sung there; how many bowls of wassail drunk!

Just as the fiefs used to cluster in the protection of the medieval castle walls, so the great house is surrounded by the thatched houses of the peons — huts of palm with the firelight of the stone ovens sparkling against the shadows of the dim interiors. An old, old church where the peons of the ranch have worshiped for generations. It has an indefinable air of serene age — rich with the memories of a life that has been lived, of generations who have been born on the ranch and have died — generation following generation — even as the sugar-cane is cut down and grows again.

In the valleys below La Puga are haciendas even more touched with medieval memories. Some are like Middle-Ages castles — stone lookout towers slit for rifle-fire; great studded gates opening into barricaded courtyards; beacon lights where watch-fires flared against the blackness of the dangers of the night. Mexico is a land of tragedy and tears, as well as gayety and song. Around every old Mexican building hangs the suggestion of dark memories — of battle and of death.

Built into the rear of the patio walls at La Puga are the shops of the ranch. There are peons who do nothing but braid rawhide into reatas; wistful-eyed, piratical-looking men with their feet in sandals, cutting innumerable steer hides into strips for thongs. There are others who make saddles and bridles and hobbles for the cow-ponies. In front of the shops is a large stone fountain where the rawhide is soaked as it is worked.

Much of the activity of this part of the establishment has to do with making ox-yokes. This is an ox country. Farther north, the oxen are nervous little creatures who weave see-saw and struggle at the yoke. The oxen at La Puga are serene, big cream-colored fellows.

My people have lived for nearly three hundred years on an old farm in New England. They still use oxen, so I know something about them. Mexican oxen are handled in an entirely different way. In place of the heavy yoke that goes over the necks of our Rhode Island oxen, the Mexicans fix their yokes in what seems a cruel way. The pole of the wagon is fastened to a straight bar of wood to which the horns of the two oxen are tightly lashed with thongs of rawhide. The result is that neither ox can move his head. The whole weight of the load comes on his forehead. American engineers who have tested it say that an ox cannot pull as much this way as with a yoke around his neck. The Mexicans cling to the old way through tradition.

The oxen themselves are a part of tradition. Their use undoubtedly began with the military invasions of the West Coast by the Conquistadores. An ox is — or was — an ideal beast of burden for a marching army. When his burden is used up, the soldiers can eat the ox. In present conditions in Mexico, the oxen are probably more useful than horses. They will patiently struggle to get a cart over a muddy, thick road where a team of horses would kill themselves plunging into the collars. The Mexicans say they are much better than any other sort of pulling animals on steep mountain roads.

In the old days of our frontier, there was developed a

mule-driver whose pride was that he could urge on his team by picturesque and colorful language. The theory, at least, was that mules were especially sensitive to the inspiration that came from swear words. The Mexican uses another method to urge his ox-team on to violent and supreme effort. He twists their tails. We came across one ox-driver who induced his beasts to impossible feats of strength by biting their tails with his teeth. To an ox there seems to be something especially inspiring about being bitten on the tail.

CHAPTER VIII
THE OLDEST CITY IN AMERICA

ONE of the two scouts reined his horse and swung his great musket into position. A corporal spurred up his horse to find out the cause of the disturbance. Together the two soldiers watched two strange figures making their way along the edge of the river. They were in tattered rags, almost naked. They were plainly starved and famished. They were dragging themselves along in the last stages of exhaustion. Neither — to the surprise of the Spanish soldiers — was an Indian. One was a white man with a long unkempt beard. The other was a coal-black Negro.

The corporal took them at once to the officer in command. To this officer they told one of the most amazing stories that was ever told to anyone in the world.

It was the year 1538: the place was just north of the present city of Culiacan, and the men were Cabeza de Vaca and a Negro slave named Estebanico. Culiacan has been the scene of many strange dramas, but the meeting of the Spanish officer and the ragged wreck of a man who held to the cavalry horse for support as he walked was the strangest.

Cabeza de Vaca is one of the greatest figures in the history of North America. He might justly and truly be called one of the Pilgrim Fathers of the United States. He explained to the Spanish officer that he had been one of an exploring expedition that had left Spain in a great ship and

had landed in Florida — about where the present city of
Tampa stands. There were six hundred men in the expedition. Their purpose was to explore and claim the new
land of America for the Spanish King. They ran into hard
luck: attacked by hostile Indians; starved; perished in
floods, and died of exposure.

In the end only four were left — Cabeza de Vaca and
the Negro slave who had been captured in his home in
Africa and sold to a Spanish soldier, and two others. For
nine terrible years they wandered through the country.
They kept on always walking toward the west. They knew
it was impossible to turn back. Somewhere toward the
setting sun, they knew there was a place called Mexico —
and in Mexico they could find their own people.

Sometimes they lived with the Indians, whom they
succeeded in making their friends. Cabeza de Vaca was a
gentleman of good education. He knew enough about
medicine to help the sick Indians. At least he knew more
than their medicine-men with their magic incantations.
But the Indians could not help them much in return. They
were on the verge of starvation most of the time. At times
the four went together. Sometimes they made their ways
separately. Most of the time Cabeza de Vaca and the
slave Estebanico traveled together. Their suffering was
horrible — ghastly. Only men with lion hearts could have
staggered on year after year — nine years.

Cabeza de Vaca was the first white man ever to cross the
American continent; the first white man ever to see a
buffalo with which the prairies at that time were covered.
No doubt you will wonder as I did how such a man came
to bear a name that — in Spanish — means 'head of a
cow.' Oddly enough, this queer name was a mark of

honor. Many years before one of his ancestors had guided
a Spanish army through a hidden cañon in Spain. In so
doing he had enabled the army to escape annihilation at
the hands of the Moors. In this cañon a conspicuous object had been the bleaching skull of a cow. So they named
the place 'E Cañon de Cabeza de Vaca.' When the King
gave a title to the guide as reward, he remembered that
cañon. That is why a brave grandee of Spain came to be
named Cabeza de Vaca — head of a cow.

Cabeza de Vaca told many strange and wonderful
stories to the Spanish officer while he was recovering his
health and strength in the garrison town of Culiacan. He
told them of a legend he had heard among the Indians.
It was the legend of the Seven Golden Cities of Cibola.

Had it not been for this legend, we might never have
had the West. This story inspired most of the early explorers. It was to search for these fabled cities that Coronado started on the journey that resulted in the discovery
of New Mexico, Arizona, the Grand Cañon, and all the
lands as far east as Kansas.

Cabeza de Vaca returned to Spain, but the Negro slave
Estebanico went back to the wild country. In company
with a brave and adventurous priest, he tried to find the
cities of Cibola. They wandered all over New Mexico and
Estebanico was clubbed to death by the Indians in the
pueblo of Zuñi — which is still there. You can see the
rock from which the priest watched the death of the black
slave. The priest escaped and came back to Mexico to tell
the officers that he thought Zuñi was one of the cities of
Cibola. The other two companions of Cabeza de Vaca
finally returned safely to Mexico.

This is but one of the dramas that have made Culiacan

historic. It is a beautiful place. We arrived there at the
end of a long day's ride through the pathway of old revolutions. Ruined haciendas, broken walls, wrecked patios,
banyan trees growing in loneliness out of adobe walls —
adobe walls that once looked down upon gay fandangos —
the lilt of Mexican music, laughter and happiness. Some
of these old haciendas have been fought over dozens of
times during the years of battle. The cattle have gone to
fill the stomachs of marching revolutionary armies.

Sunset — the blue spires of Culiacan against the tropic
sky. Culiacan is old. Incredibly and unbelievably old. It
was nearly a thousand years old when Columbus discovered America. It has been a governed city since 522.
When Culiacan was founded, our British ancestors were
trying to repel the invading Viking war parties — with
their steer-horn helmets and their terrible two-handed
swords.

Other old cities have been found in the jungles of Yucatan; but they are ruins — memories. Culiacan has been a
city — almost without interruption — for fourteen hundred years. If the people of Culiacan followed our pleasing
custom and hung the portraits of all the mayors in the City
Hall, Culiacan's first one would be shown as a half-naked
savage who gnawed his dinner off a bone.

Culiacan was started by a wandering tribe of Toltecs
coming down the coast from Alaska. They stayed about
two hundred years and wandered along to the south to
found what is now the City of Mexico. After them the
Aztecs came to Culiacan. They were more savage and
fiercer than the Toltecs. Primitive people coming from a
bitter cold climate like Alaska to a warm country nearly
always develop culture and civilization. The vitality that

has been used to keep their feet warm goes to their brain cells. After a while the Aztecs followed the Toltecs to the south, where they founded the great empire of Montezuma with superb temples, its processions of priests, and its human sacrifices.

Then the Spanish knights came from the other direction — from the south. The Spanish Conquistadores came to Mexico looking for gold. They conquered the empire of Montezuma, but they were a little disappointed in the loot. They had an idea that Montezuma's gold came from the mines on the West Coast. With almost incredible courage and energy their little armies of knights and soldiers pushed in over cruel mountain ranges; through jungles and across wild, turbulent rivers. They established frontier posts as our army did against the Indians in Dakota and Montana in the early border days. They fought for more than a hundred years for possession of the valleys around Culiacan. It was worth fighting for. They realized it was the garden spot of the world.

Sinaloa — the State of which Culiacan is the capital — is an enormous shelf of land running from a rampart of high mountains to the sea. Eleven large rivers flow across it. These mountain streams come tearing down in the spring flood, carrying great quantities of silt. As a result Sinaloa is covered with a thick carpet of soft, rich soil. The headwaters of these rivers drop over mountain cliffs in swift, sparkling cascades. Some day these waters will be put to work making electricity to drive the machinery of a new industrial Mexico.

Modern Culiacan is one of the gayest, liveliest, merriest cities in all Mexico. Two broad rivers come together just above the town. Around these rivers much of the social life of the peons transpires. The peon women do their washing on the banks of the stream. Washday — which is nearly every day — is quite a gala affair. The women build a little rough shelter of leafy boughs — called a *ramada* — at the edge of the stream. This protects them from the sun as they do the family laundry. They have no washboards. They clean the clothes by slapping them with little wooden paddles on the wet rocks. In the morning you will see scores of these laundry ramadas lining the river-banks. The women have a grand time gossiping and laughing and talking. At their work, they wear long, loose gowns like our Mother Hubbards. After they have finished the washing and hung the clothes out to dry on the ramadas or on bushes, they nearly always go in swimming in their Mother Hubbards. You see them afterward drying their long black hair as they wait for the clothes to dry — which isn't very long in that hot dry air.

They carry the clean clothes home on their heads. Mexican women always carry burdens on their heads. I have seen little girls struggling to lift a five-gallon oil-can full of water. And if you have ever tried to pick up a five-gallon can filled with water, you know that it is no light load. But with the cans balanced on the top of their heads, they walk off quite easily. These head burdens give them a very straight carriage. When I saw peon women walking along, with beautiful pottery ollas balanced on their heads, I always expected to see the ollas drop. But I have yet to see one fall. They make no special effort to maintain the balance. They just walk along easily, not even holding the ollas in place with a hand. Sometimes, when the burden is especially heavy, they wear little felt head-pads.

Culiacan is famous all over Mexico for its pretty girls.

Those of the aristocratic class live rather secluded lives, never even walking down the street without a chaperon. The girls of the peon class have more freedom. They come to the river every day to swim. It is very curious to see them afterward — getting dressed in full sight of the world, putting on the latest Hollywood clothes and shaking out their fashionable boyish bobs, indifferent as to whether or not the public is looking on.

We stayed in an old hotel which was very charming. The dining-room was an immense room open on one side to the patio, fragrant with flowers and green with banana and other tropic trees. Our bedrooms were twice the size of an ordinary bungalow living-room, with big windows. The floors were made of separate pieces of wood, like a mosaic. Long ago these floors were very fashionable. It was rather funny, because the floors squeaked as you walked.

I never got tired of sitting on the little balcony in front of my room watching the traffic flowing by. One minute it would be a company of Mexican soldiers marching stiffly along like West-Pointers to the music of drums and bugles. Mexican bugle-calls are much more beautiful than ours. Their mess-call is a wild wail that suggests a dying swan. Considering it often calls them to a meal of tortillas that they have made themselves, it seems too beautiful for the purpose.

In the trail of the soldiers will be a band of burros loaded with sugar-cane — or perhaps with earthen jars and pots and dishes. Sometimes a train of burros comes in from the ranches loaded with live chickens. The chickens are packed on burros in little wicker cages, something like bird-cages: although I have seen a burro draped all over with live turkeys — or even a pig or two.

WASHING WOMEN IN CULIACAN

There are a few automobile taxicabs; but the taxis I liked best were funny two-wheeled carts with canopies on top. There are two seats — one for you and one for the driver. They are called *arañas* (ah-rahn-yahs), which, in Spanish, means spider.

The people in Culiacan seem to dance all the time. Perhaps this is because the girls are so very lovely. There are little dancehalls down by the river. At the slightest excuse they give a fandango. Hollywood jazz dance music is, alas, more popular than their own Mexican music.

At the edge of town are little suburban settlements — what we should call crossroads. The houses have a different character from those in the northern part of Mexico. In the north, the peon houses are all of stone and adobe. As you come farther down in the hot country, many are made of what is called wattle. They make a wall by thrusting straight, hard arrowweed stalks into the ground; then another wall a few inches from it. Between the two barriers of arrowweed they pour stones and adobe. It makes an excellent house. The roofs are thatched from arrowweed and sometimes palm fronds.

The peasant houses around Culiacan are charming, as peasant houses usually are in all countries. About half the house is made of outdoors. There is one room — or maybe two — completely walled in. But standing out from this like a porch is a big ramada without walls, but with a roof of thatch. In this ramada the life of the family is carried on. Here they cook and eat and sometimes sleep.

Many Americans have come to live in Culiacan. They have haciendas back in the country. Young American boys come down as engineers and marry Mexican girls of the better class and enter into a life that is half Latin and half Anglo-Saxon — and altogether charming. We attended one of these weddings, which was performed with great elegance and gayety. But when it was over and the handsome young college boy had been married to the most beautiful señorita you ever could imagine, I heard one of the girls say — with perhaps some secret envy — 'Poor Guadalupe; she is only a Gringa now.'

CHAPTER IX

UN GRAN CABALLERO

EL SEÑOR DON ALBENO MARIA GUADALUPE RODRIGUEZ is un gran caballero. He is forty-five years old and exactly three feet, five inches tall. We did ourselves the honor to make his acquaintance in the town of Santiago the day we left Culiacan. He sat with a grand air on his tiny fawn-colored burro and informed us with a flourish, 'Esta es su ciudad.' (This is your city.) We didn't feel like packing off the city, however, although we might reasonably have done so, there being only two adobe houses. We realized that El Señor was only extending the usual charming Mexican courtesy. Whenever you go into a Mexican house, the host always says, 'Esta es su casa.' (This is your house.)

We discovered that we had been tactless in selecting this day to meet Don Albeno. It was the most unfortunate day of his life. Although he had fought in several revolutions and had been married three times, his heart was still gay for fandangos. The night before he had attended a gorgeous fandango in a neighboring town. In the course of the festivities a rival caballero had given offense. Drawing himself to his full yard and five inches, Don Albeno had challenged the contemptible interloper to fight then and there to the death. But his little squeaky voice had been lost in the music of the dance. In fact, the rival caballero — not knowing that he was being defied to come outside and be slain — had been so careless as to step on the person of El Gran Caballero, El Señor Don Albeno Maria Guadalupe Rodriguez. As though that were not mortification enough, on the way home late that night, Don Albeno had the misfortune to fall off his fawn-colored burro. Although the burrito was not much taller than a big dog, Don Albeno was too little to climb back on again. To the great disaster of his pride, he was obliged to walk all the way home leading the burro.

In his more serious moments of earning a living, Don Albeno engaged in a most heroic and sensational occupation. He caught wild horses and wild steers. This he accomplished by guile and strategy. Don Albeno found out where the wild horses came to the water-holes to drink. In these animal trails he would cunningly place the loop of a hidden lasso. The other end he tied to a tree. When the wild horse or steer came along, its legs would be caught and it would struggle until it fell all in a tangle. When it had tied itself up into a quite hopeless knot, Don Albeno would swagger out of his hiding-place, place one tiny foot on the head of the quivering monster, and laugh a laugh of contemptuous triumph.

It was dark night when we came into the mountain town of Elota. It was dirty, forlorn, and forsaken — utterly dreary. A few shabby houses on dirty streets against the dark shape of the mountains. There was no hotel. We were to be quartered in the casa of the apothecary. He had the best house in town. He had his drugstore in one of the front rooms. In this was an array of patent medicines and jars of rouge and boxes of violent-looking lipsticks for the señoritas.

When we arrived, all the élite of the town were assembled in the druggist's patio and were seated in state —

señoritas with demure, curious eyes bunched in between fat señoras. Everyone in town who had not been invited to the party crowded around the doors and windows, ten or twelve deep, their tall sombreros dim shapes in the night. The village band was just getting ready to play. The leader was giving a magnificent gesture with his cornet — preliminary to the crash of harmony that was to follow. When a most unexpected event happened.

Up dashed two automobile trucks — one filled with pretty señoritas and the other carrying a rival band. With dismay the Mayor of Elota realized the full significance — which we, at the time, did not. It meant that the rival town of San Ignacio had executed a brilliant flank movement. It seems that San Ignacio had every expectation that the Gringos would come there to spend the night instead of at Elota. Preparations had been made for a grand fandango. When no Gringos appeared, suspicion entered the heart of the Mayor of San Ignacio. He sent out a courier, who came galloping back on a spent and weary horse to announce that the Gringos were in the hands of the treacherous rival, Elota.

Dismay never enters the heart of a Napoleon. The Mayor of San Ignacio gathered up all the señoritas who had come to the fandango and hustled them into a motor truck — for the first time in their lives without chaperons. Into another truck he crowded the musicians of the village band: the two trucks tore out through the darkness for Elota.

Before he could recover his senses, the Elota bandmaster found himself outgeneraled. Before he could get his musicians launched into *Rancho Grande*, the invading band from San Ignacio was almost tooting its brains out, playing *Negra Consentida*. All night long, the band of Elota waited for a chance to show its art and talent. But every time the bandmaster of Elota lifted his cornet as a signal, the band from San Ignacio crashed into a blare of music and drowned it out.

When I went to bed that night, the fandango was still going on. But, as the night dragged on, I could hear the valiant band from San Ignacio growing weaker and weaker ... until at last just before the first light of dawn came over the mountains, the San Ignacio band gave one last despairing exhausted toot and expired.

Then, like a jungle roar, came a blast of triumph. The Elota band, which had been waiting in concealment, gave a preliminary 'Umpa, Umpa, Umpa,' and sent the echoes ringing with *Marcha Zacatecas*. The San Ignacio band could only glare in futile rage. It was down and counted out. The last sound that assailed the infuriated ears of the San Ignacio band as it sped away in the automobile truck was the Elota band playing in a most insulting manner the American jazz tune, 'Show Me the Way to Go Home.'

At Elota we had our first experience with a Mexican boarding-house. The room where I slept was also the telephone exchange. My dreams were disturbed by a señorita flying wildly in and stumbling over the furniture to plug in at the switchboard.

The bed upon which I slept was of rawhide. There were no sheets or blankets — only a thin spread — and the wind came off the mountains snows bitterly cold. In the middle of the night I had to get up and fish out a camp sleeping-bag from one of the caravan trucks. I discovered that it is the custom in all these rural inns for the parlor boarders to bring along their own serapes by way of bedclothes. I be-

gan to understand why El Norteño never parted from his.
I gave him money and he came back with a serape for me.
It was of such a bright redness that it looked like a sunset
in the act of bleeding to death. I looked like a ripe tomato
with it folded about me.

A Mexican without a serape is like a chicken without
feathers. The serape is a closely woven blanket six to
eight feet long. In the middle is a long slit through which
you can poke your head, letting the garment drape over
you, front and rear. The serape is at once the saddle-
blanket, bed-covering, and overcoat. In latter days the
cheaper serapes are made by machinery and are of cheap
red cotton; the peons usually wear such. The old hand-
wovens, like El Norteño's, have been handed down from
generation to generation. The very finest ones come from
Saltillo — capital of Coahuila. The designs are conventionalized sunsets and sometimes Aztec gods. The best for
everyday use are made in Pueblo and Oaxaca from the
wool of native sheep — usually gray and black — sometimes with the winged lion. Weavers of serapes usually
die of tuberculosis on account of the dust.

With daylight came hard realities. This is a cruel country... high, barren mountains... forlorn, heartrending
little towns. The struggle for life is pitiful and terrible. I
don't see how they live. Or on what.

One hears a great deal in the United States about 'lazy
Mexicans.' The fact is, that almost any other people —
faced with their problems — would have sunk in bitterness
and despair. I have seen whole families patiently plodding
from one end of Mexico to the other — the babies packed
on the burro — looking for work. In Guaymas I saw
scores of peons — hungry and exhausted — who had

walked for days pursuing a rumor that laborers were needed in California. Turned back, they were sleeping with their families in tents made of old bags on the cold stones on the water-front — patient, uncomplaining, sad-eyed, but accepting their fate.

The Mexican is a strong character. In his veins is the blood of the Spanish Conquistadores and the blood of dark, enduring Indian races. It will be interesting to see what new vistas of progress are opened to Mexico when the peon woman is released from her life of endless, grinding toil. It seems to me that I cannot remember to have seen an idle Mexican woman.

It is in these mountain hamlets like Elota that the lives of the women are hardest. Their work is endless. All the water used in the households has to be carried in earthen jars from the river — a quarter of a mile or more. Every river crossing is the scene of endless processions of Rebeccas going to the well. Tourists find it picturesque, but the Mexican would prefer the picturesqueness of a kitchen sink.

The pitiful little crops of corn that they raise in patches in the river bottoms must be ground by the women on their metates. The metate is a flat slab of volcanic rock. Upon this they lay the corn and grind it to a flour with a sort of stone rolling-pin. Corn has a hard, tough kernel. To crush it is hard, back-breaking work. The life of a Mexican peasant woman, from the time she is a young girl until she is old and broken with toil, is spent over a metate. Mexico's real national anthem is the pat-pat-pat of women making tortillas.

Every day is washday in Mexico. And doing the family laundry, squatting on one's knees on the wet rocks of a river, is not my idea of a joyous outdoor sport. No one knows what the future will hold for Mexico when this bitter, endless toil has been replaced by modern sanitation — the kitchen sink and the hot-water heater. Being a workhorse hasn't taken the charm from the Mexican peon women, however. They have a shy, quiet dignity that whispers of their Indian blood.

In a little town named Quila (Key-la), we swooped down on a quiet little home and asked for lunch. In our party was the Governor of Sinaloa and his staff and all these strange Gringo engineers — more celebrities than the peon woman had ever seen before in her life. There was not half enough in the house to eat. There are not many races who could have produced a woman capable of meeting the situation with such poise and composure. She was courteous, deferential, but unflustered. In the end, some of the young engineers got canned food out of the cars and invaded her kitchen. They fried bacon and eggs; made coffee, and even tried their hands at tortillas. I think we must admit that the average American woman would have been reduced to the verge of hysterics with all these strange Gringos messing around the kitchen while the Governor waited for his luncheon. She was as serene as an April morning.

CHAPTER X

A RENDEZVOUS WITH DEATH

HE WAS quite the most elegant fellow I had seen in Mexico. His army officer puttees were polished until they gleamed in the sun. His coat was a gay-colored mackinaw and his felt sombrero — decorated with silver embroidery — was cocked at an alluring angle over his handsome young face.

As he passed along the 'Street of the High Waves' (Calle de las olas altas), he gave me a glance of some dissatisfaction as though to demand a reason why a little fat Gringo should stand between him and the panorama of a glorious April morning. But he shook off the annoyance with a shrug of his shoulders; lit a cigarette; drew in a long, happy breath of fresh salt air and continued his blithe and careless stride.

Two little soldiers, who walked with him, fell behind a step or two — humbly abashed by his swaggering picturesqueness. He had the appearance of a gentleman on his way to a rendezvous. As, indeed, he was. He had a rendezvous with Death. He was on his way to be shot in front of an adobe wall in the old Spanish fort on the hill.

We waited, and the bright air of the morning seemed to strangle us as we waited — tense and nerve-strained. At last the ocean breeze brought in the faint crash of a volley of musketry, and we knew it was the end of the gay young officer with the silver-embroidered sombrero. He had in a moment of sudden passion shot a soldier with his silver-mounted revolver.

THE 'STREET OF THE HIGH WAVES,' MAZATLAN
The Cathedral in the background

Anything can happen in Mazatlan. And almost everything does. It is the most beautiful place I have seen in
any country; but it seems, somehow, like a movie set.
You always have the feeling that presently the studio
'prop' man will come along, pack it away on shelves, and
get a receipt on a printed form for the pieces.

Mazatlan is a seaport — an old 'hang-out' of pirates
and smugglers on the Gulf of California. It has religiously
followed the policy of 'Try everything once.' It has tried
everything several times. It has been fought over with
shot and shell so many times that it has lost all count. But
no tragedy has been able to take away its gayety and
charm. Once you have seen Mazatlan, it will live in
your heart forever.

There are really two Mazatlans. One flows along a sunlit street where the surf splashes over the sea-wall at high
tide, drenching the pavements with rainbow spray. This
street is like a Mexican Riviera, with sidewalk cafés,
where you sip your afternoon coffee and let your dreams
drift out to the little high-peaked islands that stand in an
azure sea; old Spanish inns; great casas whose tropic
palms peep over the balconies and garden walls.

You turn down a side street and step back four hundred
years — old churches, soft-colored with the tender touch
of age; ancient cemeteries whispering with memories; endless burro trains loaded with wood and pottery and fodder
from the mysterious mountains; islands of coconut palms;
long, sleepy lagoons where the wrecks of forgotten ships
lie half-buried in the sand; flocks of screaming parrakeets
— and everywhere the soft serenity of the tropic sun.

The hotel where we stopped was built in recent years,
but seemed very old, for it is a replica of a Spanish inn. In

the patio they kept — until lately — a huge snake, a python, to catch rats. He lay all day coiled under the palm trees, his beady little eyes contemplating the passing world without compromise. A year or so ago, he passed to Snake Paradise.

In the American Consulate on the 'Street of the High Waves,' I found a quaint old book which told of past days — past comedies and tragedies. It was a file copy of all the letters written about a hundred years ago. In those days, having no typewriters and no carbon paper, they had to copy all their letters 'by hand' in a record-book. These letters were written by the American Consul at Mazatlan to Daniel Webster, who was at that time Secretary of State. The Consul was finding the job so filled with difficulty and high drama that he was always threatening to resign.

One day he wrote a hurried letter which sizzled with excitement. A British man-of-war had anchored in the harbor and a Mexican clerk from the office of the port captain had not watched his manners. He had offended the dignity of His Britannic Majesty's Royal Navy by being — as we say — 'sassy.' Whereupon the British captain had returned to his ship and had notified the Mexican Government that he would procced to bombard the town; just blow it into flinders and toothpicks — if that clerk didn't come right out and apologize.

Our agitated Consul was writing to inform Daniel Webster that the sassy clerk said he would be gosh-dinged if he would apologize. The guns were loaded; the captain was walking the quarter-deck in high indignation, and goodness knows what was going to happen.

Another letter — that almost seemed to sigh with relief out of the yellowed old pages — announces that the sassy clerk decided to apologize; so nobody was blown into toothpicks or flinders and the crimson banners of the British Empire still floated with pride at the masthead.

Another letter tells the Secretary of State about a deed of great heroism which earned the gratitude of the United States. There had been a hurricane — one of the storms which sometimes tear in from the Gulf in wild fury. The harbor of Mazatlan has a rock bottom with very little mud; so the anchors do not hold very well. In this hurricane every ship in the harbor had been lost. With almost incredible courage and strength a Mexican fisherman had rowed his little boat in the teeth of the storm and had rescued five American sailors. The Consul suggested to Daniel Webster that the honor and dignity of the United States Government demanded that the man be suitably rewarded. For his valor in risking his life to save the sailors, he ought to be given three pesos (about a dollar and a quarter). But inasmuch as he lost an oar, the Consul thought that a grateful Republic ought to give him another two pesos for the oar — making a magnificent total of about three dollars. Presumably the money was paid, as nothing more was said about the matter. I hope that this sudden avalanche of wealth did not ruin the man's character.

At the edge of the old part of town is an ancient cemetery, hidden by a high brick wall adorned with much fancy decoration and ironwork. In this cemetery the bodies of the dead are lowered into rented graves. They are rented for a period of five years. If the rent is not forthcoming at the end of that time, the bones are thrown out and there is a vacant grave for rent. This seemed horrifying to us, but the Mexicans do not look at Death as we do. They face it with a shrug of indifference — like the young officer on the 'Street of the High Waves.' Death comes to all — now or later.

One day we saw a little girl's funeral in Mazatlan. It was a gala affair. Out from the top of the little white hearse stretched long white ribbons, the ends of which were held by little girls in white lawn dresses. They walked by the side of the hearse. As they held out the white ribbons it was exactly like a Maypole dance.

The hearse was followed by an automobile carrying the priest and the mourners — the little girl's father and mother. On the back of this automobile was a big sign which said:

TONIGHT!　TONIGHT!

CHARLIE CHAPLIN

IN

'THE CIRCUS'

They didn't mean to be heartless. It was only that death is an everyday affair in Mexico.

It is a common sight at Mazatlan — as in nearly all Mexican cities — to see a sad-eyed peon walking along with his broken-hearted little wife, carrying a tiny coffin on his head. Sometimes these baby coffins are covered with silver or gold paper. Often the coffin is just a pitiful little black box. The people are very poor and cannot afford to hire a hearse. But it was pitiful to see how wistfully one little mother watched — as she followed a little black coffin on her husband's head — the white hearse going by with the Maypole white ribbons and the flowers.

But Mazatlan is not all death and war. It is, in fact, a

very gay, lively, little town. About twice a week a steamer stops in the harbor on its way from California or New York or Cuba. For four or five hours Mazatlan is filled with tourists intent on buying souvenirs. They buy Mexican sandals, perfumes, and baskets. Very few young lady tourists leave Mazatlan without a pair of iguana shoes. An iguana is a horribly ugly lizard which infests all this part of Mexico. Sometimes it grows five or six feet long and looks like a spirit of evil. It is harmless; is found in all tropical America, eaten, and tastes like tender chicken. When skinned, its hide makes the most beautiful shoe leather. A great many so-called snakeskin shoes and purses and girls' 'aviator hats' are made of the soft, pliable hides of the giant lizards of Mexico.

Mazatlan is also a division point on the railroad. Nearly all the engineers and brakemen and dispatchers and porters are Mexicans. The trains stop for nearly an hour there, so the station platforms are like public markets — Mexican women selling tamales and fruit and baskets and souvenirs. They stay until late at night and the old-fashioned flaming kerosene torches with which they light their booths give a charming flavor of picturesqueness to the scene.

But just as everywhere in Mexico the new jostles elbows with the very old, so the country beyond the railroad station circles through the hills into the country of the bandits — the wild mountains.

I had the honor of an invitation to spend two weeks as the guest of one of the most famous bandits in Mexico; I regret that I sent my 'regrets.' The bandit was a gay humorous rascal named Marcos Diaz. He was a sort of Mexican Robin Hood.

Don Marcos had a friend who was a friend of mine.
He was an American — this friend — and owned a gold
mine back in the hills. The fact that Don Marcos liked
and admired the American very much did not interfere
with his business life. Every so often he would appear at
the mine with his gang of armed men and loot the place.
Sometimes he carried away money. Sometimes all he
wanted was horses or burros, or even pack-saddles. Once
he arrived with a demand for chicken-wire fence.

Finally, the Mexican commander of Mazatlan decided
that Don Marcos was — as we say — 'getting too fresh.'
In some way the bandit had offended the dignity of the
Mexican army. The comandante sent word to El Señor
Bandido that he was commanded to come into town and
be shot in front of an adobe wall.

'Ho, ho,' replied Marcos. 'Come out and catch me if
you can.'

He should have known better. The next day the comandante sent another courier into the mountains with this
message: 'I have captured your grandmother, your
mother, and your four little children. I am going to shoot
one of them each day until you come in and surrender.
I shall begin with your grandmother.'

Don Marcos rode in that night and surrendered to the
commander, to be shot. He said something in Spanish
that might be roughly translated: 'Well, I guess the laugh
is on me.'

They made grand preparations for shooting Marcos.
They arranged to have a barbecue and sent out engraved
invitations to the party. Don Marcos took the liveliest
interest in the proceedings. He was, so to speak, all
swelled up over his own importance. At the last minute

— owing to political complications — they decided not
to shoot him, after all. I shall always think that Don
Marcos was a little bit disappointed.

After being set free, he mounted his bronco and rode
back to his American friend at the mine. He was very
reproachful.

'Now look at what you have done to me,' he said.
'You've gone and busted up my business. All my bandits
have scattered.'

'Well, that's just too bad,' said the American sarcasti-
cally. 'It looks as though you will have to go to work or
starve.'

The countenance of Don Marcos brightened at once.
This was a new idea. Work would be quite a delightful
novelty.

'Oh, yes — of a certainty,' he said. 'That will be fine.
You shall give me a job here at the mine.'

'What kind of job shall I give you?'

Don Marcos relapsed into deep thought as he studied the
problem. At last his eyes lighted up. 'After all,' he said,
'my main experience has been carrying money. You shall
give me a job carrying your money from the bank in
town to your mine. This will assure that no wicked bandit
gets it.'

At last accounts his friend was still thinking it over.
He told me he felt inclined to give Don Marcos the job.

CHAPTER XI

A PRAYER BY A ROADSIDE

WE HAD stopped for a basket luncheon near a little road-side cross. It was worn and weather-beaten. At the foot of the cross was a pile of small stones. I noticed that El Norteño picked up a little stone and placed it carefully with the other stones. He made the sign of the cross on his forehead and breast, and I could see that he was saying a prayer.

'What's the idea?' I asked him.

'I was saying a little prayer for the repose of his soul.'

'But why did you put a stone at the foot of the cross?'

'To show that I had said a prayer for the repose of his soul.'

'Who was he?'

'Quien sabe.' (Who knows?)

Then El Norteño told me that all these crosses marked the spots where someone had died by violence. Every wayfarer stops to say a prayer for the repose of the soul hurled thus suddenly — and with no priests to hear his last confession — into Eternity.

I remembered that all day we had been passing these little crosses by the roadside. Some were very old and almost covered by piled-up stones.

'Did you say that each one of these crosses marks the place where someone died?' I asked Norteño.

'Si, señor — todas.' (Yes, sir — all.)

'How is it that so many died violent deaths?'

'Bandits, some of them. Some were killed in the revolutions. People die where they die.'

I tried to take the scared strain out of my voice as I asked, as gayly as possible: 'And these bandits? They are, of course, all gone now?'

El Norteño turned with a look of surprise. 'Did you not hear me talking to those soldiers we passed? Yesterday the bandits captured an American mining-man. He had talked too much about his money. It is not well to talk too much about money, señor. He said he wanted to buy some mining claims. He hired a guide to take him back into the heart of the lonely and desolate mountains. The guide led him into the clutches of a gang of bandits. They rode out of the underbrush — four of them — and leveled guns at him. They made him ride away with them.'

'Where is he now?' I asked, with a laugh that I am afraid sounded a little nervous.

'Quien sabe?' said El Norteño indifferently. 'Somewhere up there in the mysterious mountains.'

'Will they kill him?'

'Quien sabe?' said El Norteño, who was beginning to lose interest in the subject.

We were to hear much of this case during the days that followed — but not as much as was heard in the United States. As a matter of cold fact, there are more bandits in a city like Los Angeles in one night than in the entire Republic of Mexico in a year. But being more picturesque, every bandit in Mexico becomes an alluring drama to the Yankee newspapers.

South of Mazatlan we had entered the real tropics. The imaginary line called the Tropic of Cancer that divides

the tropical zone from the north temperate zone runs
about thirty-five miles north of Mazatlan. It is the palm
country. You see great forests of palm trees. The huts
of the peons are all made of thatched palm leaves. Parrots
and strange tropical birds fly through the trees. One bird
has a very long tail that streams out like a pennant as
he flies. In a high wind these birds are blown around as
though these long tails were sails. Alligators sun themselves on the banks of slow, muddy streams. Life is crude
and primitive. In the lush lands of the river bottoms you
see peons plowing with oxen and crooked sticks for plows.
From time to time we passed little towns on the banks of
the rivers. The banks were always lined with the ramadas
of the peon women doing their daily laundry. And nearly
always we saw water-carts — a barrel with two wagon-
wheels and drawn by a mule. These carts were driven
into little towns back in the hills and the water sold at so
much a bucket. One curious thing we noticed about all
the houses: all of them had platforms upon which they
placed all their grain and hay — this because of the rats
and myriad insects of the tropics. The burros and oxen
and mules stood under the platforms and ate the hay as
it edged down between the slats of the platform.

The traffic along the country roads was quaint and
picturesque. Sometimes we passed big two-wheeled carts
with enormously high wheels, drawn by six or seven oxen.
Sometimes we saw what in our own border days of the
West were called 'spike teams'.— four burros harnessed
in a line at the wheel; two or three burros harnessed in
front of them. The effect was of a wedge-shaped — or
spike-shaped — team. Sometimes the wagon-wheels were
so high and the burros were so little, it looked as though

the wagon would run right over them. They were like a lot of little chickens with the high wagon for an old hen.

The chief crops raised in this part of Mexico are sugar-cane and bananas.

We stopped that day for a while at an old town, Rosario. The whole town is built over a mine. The Tajo Mine is probably the oldest producing mine on the American continent. It has been in active operation for more than three hundred years. The tradition is that, way back in the days of the Spanish Conquistadores, a party of soldiers were marching north along the West Coast. As was usual, they had a band of live cattle with them for food. To take care of these cattle they had a vaquero. They made camp at the present site of Rosario. The vaquero built a little fire and cooked his dinner by himself. In the morning he noticed that on the ground where the hot embers had been were little hunks of melted gold and silver.

A town grew up around the mine; then a very beautiful church. With the exception of one or two I have seen farther south in Mexico, it is the loveliest Spanish church I know. It is built in the Spanish Colonial style, with a golden altar, two belfrys, one above the other. From the ground beside the great door a caracol stairway runs all the way up to the bells and the choir loft.

The entrance to the mine is right in the middle of the town. Through the years they burrowed out tunnels until the tunnels completely undermine the streets and the houses. The weight of the old church is so great that it has begun to settle into the underground workings. One of the walls leans over perilously, and huge cracks have riven the nave. The American engineers in charge of the mine told me, however, that they have been able to reënforce the structure so that the devastation will go no farther.

These young American college boys in charge of the work told me that, in tunneling, they come across old engineering works made by Spanish engineers of the days of the Conquest. Considering the crude tools they had, they were wonderful engineers. There is nothing that modern engineers could tell them about taking out ore or treating it. The only thing they didn't know, that moddern engineers know, is about the new metals that have been discovered.

Puffing around the town were two little engines drawing trains of ore cars from the mine to the smelters. There seemed something strangely familiar about them. I learned that they used to be in the Chutes Amusement Park in San Francisco — giving rides to excited, shrieking children.

Just before darkness fell that night, we drove through a giant palm forest so dense that the light filtered through only in wan patches. Even at noonday it was dark; late in the afternoon it was like a tomb. Its blackness was creepy and mysterious. Right in the middle of the forest we found a clearing where a few Indians lived in a town where the houses were all made of palm leaves. They were, in reality, little more than thatched roofs with one wall or no walls. It is always summer there and so hot that they do not need houses — except to keep off the rain. These Indians made their living by gathering nuts. We made a call of ceremony and state at the house of the head man who kept his pig under his bed.

Finally — just at dusk — we came out of the forest into a valley where the road skirted the dark jungle. The soldiers had left us a long way back. With us, however, was an automobile filled with officers of the State Police. They were picturesque, handsome fellows, with velvet waistcoats and revolvers, whose holsters eclipsed all the other decorated holsters we had seen in point of elegance.

They signaled for the caravan to stop and came back to our cars.

'See that your revolvers are fully loaded,' they said. 'Each man who sits next to the driver must carry a rifle and see that it is loaded and ready for action. We are getting into the bandit country.'

When it grew really dark with the thick, heavy darkness of the tropics, we turned on the headlights of the cars. The caravan was stopped again. The officers came back to tell us that, on no account, must we show any lights. They said that we should be a target for bandit shots if we showed lights in the midst of the night. It was grand melodrama, but we got tired of banging along on a dark road — so we turned on the lights. Personally I believe we were safer than we should have been in any large American city.

'Now,' they said, 'all the cars must keep right together. Be sure not to lose sight of our car.' Whereupon they stepped on the gas; sped away with a rush and roar — so fast that we did not see them again.

El Norteño here really began to live. He stationed himself on the running-board of our car and never left it during the long night ride, clinging there like a monkey. He was armed like a deep-sea pirate: two bandoleers of belted cartridges over his shoulders; an enormous American cavalry revolver and a Winchester rifle. He was all in favor of battle.

Afterward we discovered that we had packed all of our own ammunition somewhere back in the baggage-car with the canned tomatoes. Had we met any real bandits, our cartridges would probably have been of as much value among the canned goods as in our guns.

I have been asked very often as to the truth about Mexican bandits. Well, then, the truth is this:

Nayarit is a wild country of mysterious mountain fastnesses. A few years ago these mountains contained bands of roving freebooters who maintained a sort of Robin Hood kingdom. There was one fellow who lived the life of a bandit king. He had a large hacienda back in the hills from which he sent out his forays to collect ransom.

During my first visits to Mexico, the trains from Mazatlan to Guadalajara always had armored cars and soldiers. There are no armored cars on the trains now — Mexico is safer than any modern American city.

After Obregon and Calles came into power, a savage war of extermination was started against the Al Capones of Mexico. The bandits were hunted down with cavalry — war-worn experienced troopers — and it was a war without quarter, with only little piles of stones by the roadside.

The most effective work in this blood-thirsty man-hunt was done — not by soldiers — but by spies. In bandit-chasing, the Mexican police devised a means of fighting them with spies.

One spy became very famous and effective. His plan was to turn bandit and join one of the famous gangs. Among his accomplishments was that he was a remarkably skillful knife-fighter.

It should be explained that knife-fighting is an intricate

and subtle art. El Norteño always laughed when he saw a knife-fight in a movie, with the actors holding on to each other's wrists and pumping their arms about like windmills. What especially drew giggles from El Norteño was that the movie actors always held their knives upside down. A real knife-fighter holds his Bowie as a foil-fencer holds his sword — with the forefinger extended along the handle. On his left arm by way of a guard he wraps his serape. If he has no serape he holds his sombrero. With this he knocks away the other fellow's knife when he tries to thrust. An old trick of knife-fighters is suddenly to slap the other fellow in the face with his hat. So skillful do the Mexican knife-fighters become that it is almost impossible to hurt them. I know of a case where two Mexicans fought with knives in the old Plaza in Los Angeles. They fought until the serapes wrapped around their arms were cut to shreds of yarn. They fought until they were so tired that they both fell down and could not get up. The fight lasted four hours, yet neither was scratched.

Well, this spy was the best knife-fighter in all Mexico. He would ride around with these bandits on their raids for weeks at a time, pretending to be one of them. Then one day he would manage to pick a quarrel with the leader. They would fight, and the spy always killed the bandit.

One time the spy, after gaining the complete confidence of a bandit gang, arranged a big fandango to celebrate his own or somebody's birthday. When the bandits came to the party — suspecting nothing — the spy gave a signal and concealed soldiers shot them to death.

In the large cities of Mexico, the criminal element was wiped out by methods that offer a suggestion to Chicago.

A handsome young fellow of good family — Roberto Cruz by name — became chief of police. He introduced the grim 'Law of Flight,' where every known gangster was assumed — on being arrested — to have attempted to escape. One morning a grim news item appeared in a Mexican paper to the effect — 'Last night the inmates of a known den of crime unfortunately got into a quarrel and they all killed each other.' In two months the thugs of Mexico City were dead or on the way to the United States, where they could have the protection of slush funds, shyster lawyers, and complacent courts.

It was late at night when we crawled into a little country inn at the old, old town of Acaponeta. We took a walk around the town — the Plaza with its dilapidated grandstand, long rows of adobe houses, and a big stone cathedral. We heard a tragic and terrible story about this old church.

Owing to a dispute with the Mexican Government, the priests were all compelled to leave Mexico. For a year or so the people worshiped in the churches alone as best they could — usually under the guidance of some old woman. During this period the bandits broke loose around Acaponeta. They came riding boldly into the town, of which they took full possession. The frightened people fled into the jungles or concealed themselves in their houses. About three hundred women took refuge in the church, where they knelt in prayer while the bandits rode around the town yelling and shooting.

Suddenly the front door was wrenched open and a villainous-looking bandit rode into the church on horseback. At one end of the church was a magnificent altar, built hundreds of years ago. High up on the altar was a figure of the Virgin Mary, mother of Jesus Christ. Grateful women had, during the years, hung precious ornaments on this figure. They would pray, and when their prayers were answered, they would show their gratitude by sacrificing their most precious jewels, necklaces and so on. The figure was blazing with jewels.

It caught the eye of the bandit. Riding his horse inside the altar rail, he took out his lasso and whirled it around his head. The women saw what he intended to do. He was going to lasso and drag down the jeweled figure of the Virgin from the altar. One of the women gave a terrible shriek; leaped to her feet; rushed at the bandit; climbed up the side of the horse, and clutched his throat. Instantly he was attacked from all sides. The three hundred women dragged him from the saddle — three hundred strong infuriated women, their work-worn hands given ten times their strength by hysterical fury. His horse bolted in terror down the long aisle. Tangled in the coils of his reata, the bandit was literally torn to pieces.

This, at least, is the story that is told. If it isn't all true it ought to be. It's a good one.

CHAPTER XII

AN OLD PIRATE PORT

'THE Bells of San Blas' was the last poëm written by Henry W. Longfellow. As a matter of fact, the poet never saw the place. His poetic fervor was fanned into verse by a friend who had stopped in to see the old pirate port while on a sea trip up the West Coast. Had it been vouchsafed Longfellow to have spent a few days in those quaint old streets, his poem would have been a glowing epic. For the bells of San Blas whisper of blood and tragedy, battle and treasure. Ghosts of stately galleons float on the sand-clogged lagoons; wraiths of long trains of pack-mules, weighted with gold and silks and precious spices, climb the forgotten treasure-trail built by the Conquistadores across the mountains. Memories of padres outfitting ships and expeditions for the relief of the half-starved missions and garrisons of California, memories of pirate battles that stained the quiet waters.

San Blas is a feeble old grandmother now — muttering to herself in the sun — but she has lived. She flourished in the days of the Filipino galleons. These treasure-ships were the most magnificent vessels that ever sailed the sea. Standing high out of water with great poop-decks rising like castled towers from the sea, they were regal and imperial in their grandeur. Their great sails were painted; their tall sides rose from the blue water in a gleam of gold leaf from which shone the muzzles of brass cannon. The sun sparkled on the polished armor of the soldier guard walking his post on the high quarter-deck.

The captain was always a grandee of Spain who dined in solitary grandeur and dignity in his palatial salon from plates of solid gold — like an emperor. Smaller craft scuttled out of the way of these galleons in awe and terror like a little dog slinking from the path of a St. Bernard.

By arrangement of the Spanish Government, a galleon set sail from Manila once a year bound for Mexico. She breasted the sea, hull-down with a cargo of treasure, of a value that staggers the imagination: silks from China, spices from India, gold bullion, silver plate, argots of ore packed into the great holds like ballast. They were bound for Mexico, mostly for Acapulco, but sometimes for San Blas. The fact that the Spanish built a paved treasure-road from San Blas across the mountains to Vera Cruz indicates that the commerce of this port must have been considerable.

The pirates who left bloodstains on the rocks of San Blas were almost as de luxe as the ships they attacked. They were quite elegant fellows. I am sure they would have been shocked to the distinguished marrow of their bones to have heard coarse ditties about Yo-ho and a bottle of rum: not to mention their probable horror at frivolous musical mention of a dead man's chest.

The pirate of romance and tradition was a rough person, with his cutlass between his teeth, half-boots made thick for wading around on blood-soaked decks, a scarlet kerchief around his snaky locks, and a heart hungry for murder. Of such was the pirate of the Caribbean. He was a murderer and a drunken marauder. His crew was culled from the riff-raff of the gutter — thieves, criminals, murderers, human scum. His rule was that of ferocity and terror. The strongest bully ruled. With the skull and crossbones floating from the masthead the pirates descended upon the helpless town — slew and pillaged and tortured. Afterward there was always a mad drunken brawl, with bloody fights over the division of the loot; greedy hands that reached for gold lying clinched in pools of blood.

The story of the Filipino galleons must almost be told with the story of Sir Francis Drake. He was the perfect type of the gentleman pirate — as the galleons were the perfect type of the treasure-ship of romance. Drake was an English sea captain, a quiet, self-controlled gentleman who ruled his crew with decorum and etiquette. He was probably the finest sailor and navigator of his time — one of the truly great sailors of all time. He was a pious Churchman who always had prayers said on deck before sending his pirate crew swarming into the rigging of the great Spanish treasure-ship. Although nearly always carrying off his lootings with a 'This-hurts-me-more-than-it-does-you, Sir,' he was unable to restrain his proper indignation with the captain of one galleon because of his lack of etiquette in firing a broadside at the Golden Hind before the English crew had finished its battle-prayers. That seems to have been the only time he is known to have sunk a galleon in any but the most charming manner. Even his prisoners have left diaries in which they agree that his manners were faultless. No one before or since has ever known how to slit a throat or sink a ship with more suavity or punctilio.

The best manuals and correspondence courses inform us as to the practical value of good manners in business. Witness the case of Sir Francis Drake. Being an eminently practical person, he did not bother about the filthy little loot and the pieces of eight and the golden doubloons over which the blood-thirsty thugs of the Caribbean murdered each other. Where these drunken scum got pennies, Sir Francis got pounds and golden treasure. His well-disciplined crews fought like trained bull terriers — not like gutter curs. His victories over the great Spanish galleons with their fighting men in armor form one of the astounding chapters of history. When the tiny Golden Hind sailed up to challenge a Filipino galleon, it must have looked like a fox terrier barking at an elephant. But so skillfully and bravely did his men fight as they swarmed up the golden sides and into the rigging that they seldom lost their prey. Once the proud banner of scarlet-and-gold was cut down from the masthead, the English pirate became a kindly, tactful, and considerate victor.

Drake sailed home at last with more loot than the old-fashioned pirates of the Spanish Main ever dreamed was in the world. It is related that from the wreck of one galleon, Drake took what would have amounted — in modern money — to about $15,000,000. He looted ships and Spanish colonial towns until the Golden Hind wallowed hull-down in the sea from her load of treasure. On one occasion he had to order the crew to dump overboard great deck-loads of precious cargo to make way for richer loot. Instead of the wild drunken battles over the division of the loot — as in the bloody dramas of the Caribbean — Drake distributed the shares to his men with the solemn decorum and impartiality of the directors of the First National Bank declaring a semi-annual dividend. For years, he waylaid and fought the galleons of Spain. Some of them he sent to the bottom, where the fish no doubt give Sunday afternoon excursions to peer in at the beautifully carved windows to the gold-leafed magnificence of their cabins. Other galleons, gutted like a canned fish, lived to limp into some near-by harbor, shattered and broken in their pride.

San Blas became a port of refuge into which they scuttled like badly frightened old cows seeking succor from wolves. For this reason — and for other reasons — San Blas was at one time one of the most important cities of the new world. It lies at the mouth of the Santiago River, not far from the historic towns of Tepic and Compostella. At one time it had a population of more than thirty thousand. It had a great foundry for the manufacture of church bells; wharves, custom-houses, warehouses, churches, soldier barracks, and a fort that overlooked the entrance of the bay. Nothing remains now but a handful of old houses surrounding a shabby public square. And dreams — dreams. I have seen no other town in Mexico so redolent of the past, of houses that seemed so to whisper stories.

There is a very lovely old church fronting the plaza, small but perfect. From its belfry the bells of San Blas still send out their silver chimes — just as Longfellow imagined them. The church stands on a sleepy, empty street fronted by the crumbling wrecks of old palaces with balconies and barred windows. One of these must have been a place of consequence, possibly the palace of the comandante. It has still an air of ancient hauteur. What remains of an old street-car line wanders crazily on rusted, crooked rails to the water-front — over ties cut from solid mahogany.

Half a dozen peons, with white cotton pants almost as wide as a woman's skirt, sit around the little corner store.

Once San Blas was a great fishing port, but the day we were there, the proprietor of the corner store could provide only canned salmon from Oregon. He was finally persuaded to have his wife pat some tortillas, but he was not in a lather of emotion about it. He drew some sad-looking pop-bottles out of his refrigerator — which was a block of lava rock, contributed by a prehistoric volcano in the vicinity. Holes had been bored into this rock and the bottles nested in the holes.

After luncheon, we walked down the old railroad track to the ancient port of the galleons. There isn't much left to the harbor now. For two or three hundred years, the river has been pouring silt into the lagoon until the channel is choked. Only small fishing-boats can drift through the sandbars up the river to the alligator jungles above. Across the stream you can see the remains of the old fort on the hill under whose frowning bronze cannon the galleons once took refuge. Only a few crumbling walls now mark the place. Only the old custom-house remains: it still does business. It looks like a block-house of our own frontier days, wide balconies encircling its upper story. I imagine it has been patched and rebuilt many times since its uniformed officials hurried out to board the last galleon. In the street behind it, at its four corners, are four very old brass cannon planted contemptuously — muzzle-down in the ground — to serve meekly as posts. Local tradition says that they were taken from a pirate ship which perished from over-ambition under the bellowing guns of the fortress.

The main street of San Blas was the beginning of one of the most famous highways in the whole world. It was the Spanish treasure-road, paved with tiny cobblestones, fitted together like a mosaic. It ran for countless miles over hot tropic plains and through the high mountains — flanked with stone fences piled by the patient toil of Indian slaves. This was the old Spanish treasure-road. One end was at San Blas: the other on the East Coast of Mexico, across the mountains at Vera Cruz. When the galleons landed at San Blas, the treasure cargoes were packed on mules and, under heavy military guard, started on the long, perilous journey across Mexico. At Vera Cruz, the mules delivered their pack-loads to other ships which sailed for Spain. For days we bumped along over what remains of this old Spanish treasure-road in our motor cars.

What remains of San Blas nestles up against a range of hills, covered with thick jungle growth. Hidden in the lonely silence of this jungle is the grave of another chapter of history. And this chapter belongs in greater degree to California than to Mexico.

You wind up a steep hillside trail: then plunge down into the jungle. It is so dense that the sun filters through in a wan, pale filigree of light. Fighting your way along a dim burro path, you come at last to a majestic ruin. It is the ruin of an old monastery. It looks English rather than Spanish. Out of the ruined stillness, you expect to hear the ghost of Richard Cœur-de-Lion bellowing a ballad. Yet the knights that it housed were knights of the Cross rather than knights in armor. It was the home of the priest, Fray Junípero Serra, during the period he was outfitting the expedition that was to establish the long chain of mission churches down the length of the Camino Real in California.

The roof of the old monastery has fallen in. The nave

is a mass of fallen timbers and masonry overgrown with jungle plants. At the top of one wall, which probably supported a bell-tower, a banyan tree has found life. Its long blanched roots stream hungrily down the great stone wall to the ground. I think, at that, there must have been a still earlier church, for scratching off the green mould of the jungle, we found a date, which was carved about seventy years after Father Serra landed in California, on his mission to carry the Cross to the heathen.

Plowing our way back through the jungle, we came to a fork of the trail. We came to a headland where the remains of a pretentious stone building still stand. According to tradition, this building was once the headquarters of Portola, who commanded the military end of Serra's expedition. Had it not been for these mouldering buildings, now strangled by the jungle, there would have been no California. At any rate, not a California claimed by Spain and held by Spain until Uncle Sam was ready to take it over. During the middle years of Father Serra's work among the California Indians, the Mexican Government proposed to close the port of San Blas. Father Serra made the long, agonizing trip to the City of Mexico (he suffered for years from an open sore on his leg which made riding a torture). He told the Viceroy that, if he closed the Port of San Blas, it would be necessary to abandon all the missions of California and yield the land to Russia or England. All the supply ships which at that period carried food and other necessaries to the missions outfitted at San Blas. Nearly all the mission bells which tolled the Indian neophytes to service and to their labors were moulded in a long-ago-forgotten foundry in the town of San Blas.

San Blas has written many other chapters into the history of California and the West. In 1818, the pirate-insurgent, Captain Hippolyte Bouchard, ravaged the coast of California, attacking the ranches and looting the towns, even plundering the old mission at San Juan Capistrano on the modern San Diego to Los Angeles highway. In response to a frantic appeal to the Motherland, an army of one hundred infantrymen was recruited at San Blas and one hundred cavalry from Mazatlan. They came to the rescue in troop-ships. But, before they arrived, Bouchard had sailed away. Having been recruited from the scum of a seaport town, the San Blas infantrymen became such a collective nuisance that California wailed to be delivered from the deliverers.

Later, one Manuel Micheltoreno, having been appointed Governor of California in the face of one of the current revolutions, recruited an army in San Blas that is still known to history as the 'cholo army.' It consisted of half-starved vagabonds who — according to tradition — disembarked at San Diego without the usual adornment of pants!

As late as 1840, San Blas figured in California history. Governor Juan Bautista Alvarado, having decided that the Gringo population were a pest, herded them to the number of sixty into a ship and packed them off to San Blas. The story is too long to tell, but it is a colorful chapter.

Very few tourists have visited San Blas. I don't know why. It can be reached without difficulty by sea — from yachts. It is not a specially difficult trip by motor car from the old town of Tepic. For mystery, charm, memories, I know of no place in Mexico more appealing.

CHAPTER XIII

IN OLD TEPIC

THE sad-eyed little peon and his wife were packed like two burros. He had a long board balanced on his head and the board was loaded from one end to the other with pottery. It looked as though he were walking along with a curio store on his head. His pretty little wife came pattering along the country road behind him with an enormous load of sugar-cane stalks on her back.

A bright idea struck one of the engineers. We all wanted to buy pottery. Why not buy this fellow's whole load off the plank on his head? There was a railroad station near by. We could take the stuff over there; ship it by express. Then we should not have to worry any more about our shopping. This was applauded as a grand inspiration.

El Norteño was detailed to strike the bargain. We saw him talk for a few moments to the pottery carrier. Then to our surprise the peon emphatically shook his head, hoisted his load, and dog-trotted off down the dusty road as though he were intent on escaping.

'He doesn't want to sell it all,' explained El Norteño.

'What's he got it for, then? Is this just the way he takes his daily dozen? Trotting up and down the road with a pottery store on his head?'

'He wanted to sell some of it,' said El Norteño, patiently ignoring the sarcasm. 'He is very poor and he needs the money; but he doesn't want to sell all of it.'

'What's the idea?'

'Because, if he sold all of it, there would be no reason for him to go to the market.'

This was a few miles out of Tepic. After we saw the public market there, we rather sympathized with the peon. We didn't wonder then that he liked to go. Going to market with things to sell is about all the pleasure he gets out of life.

Of all the towns in Mexico, I like Tepic the best. It is very old. It sits there, sweet and complacent and contented, while the rest of the world tears around in such a hurry that it is like a chicken with its head cut off. Tepic stands on a great plateau high in the mountains — so the weather is always cool in the hottest part of summer. In the days when Porfirio Diaz was President of Mexico, it was a favorite summer resort for the aristocracy, who came up from their haciendas in the moist hot lands of the valleys.

Back of the town — toward the Church of the Cross — is what remains of the paseo where fashionable folk used to go. The paseo was — and is — a round plaza. At the hour of sunset — and on into the evening — the Mexican belles would come out there in their open carriages with prancing horses and silver-mounted harness. Sitting demure and in an elegance of white lawn dresses, with high jeweled combs in their jet-black hair, they rode around and around the plaza. As they rode, a procession of fashionable young bachelors walked around and around the plaza in the other direction; so they were always passing and repassing. The young men in their silver-embroidered sombreros and their tight-fitting jackets were quite open in their admiration. But it was etiquette for the lovely señoritas to pretend not to notice that they were being looked at. Nevertheless, they continued to ride around and around.

The paseo is grass-grown and deserted now. The procession of fashion stopped when the Revolution swept over Mexico twenty years ago and the rich families became poor and fled to California to live. Many a happy family in Los Angeles dates back to a sidelong glance at a handsome boy from a girl in a gleaming carriage at the paseo in Tepic. The paseo will never have that procession again. Automobiles and a leisurely procession around and around a little plaza do not 'jell,' so to speak.

Everything in Mexico is a little bit mysterious, and one of the most charming mysteries at Tepic is sheltered behind a crumbling old wall, in front of the Church of the Cross, near the paseo. Inside this wall is a huge cross growing in the soil. It is made of green plant life that grows in the form of a perfect cross in the midst of a big patch of lighter-colored grass. No one knows when it first grew there — or how. All that they know is that it has been there as long as the oldest man can remember. The grass grows there, year after year, and the plant grows; but it never loses its shape or form. The Mexican people contend that it was never planted by the hand of man and that it has various miraculous powers.

The center of the town of Tepic is a public plaza four or five blocks long, fronting a fine old church with very tall belfry towers. For blocks along the streets that line this plaza and slipping into narrow side streets are the public markets. Every Saturday the peasants come in from the country to sell their wares — sugar-cane, pottery, guarachas, toys, sombreros, candy, ribbons, tamales, queer tropic fruits, baskets, horsehair bridles, reatas...

What impressed us was the quietude. Had that been an Italian or a French market, you could have heard the chatter for a mile. These Mexican-Indian women sit there on the ground — silent and watchful. They make no attempt to 'ballyhoo' their wares. There is no bargaining and no heckling — composed, inscrutable, and patient.

They may look dumb, but they are not. Those inscrutable masks cover a shyness that is Indian — and a sense of ridicule that is devastating — also Indian.

The Indian women who sit like lumps on the station platforms at Albuquerque and Yuma go back to their homes to mimic the passengers they have seen — and to cry for hours over the smart cracks of the hosiery drummers.

In their own homes these silent Mexican peon women are gay, sarcastic, voluble. A quarrel between two of them fills the air with language.

Mexican women of the upper classes talk in streams in the home circle — nobody listening to anyone else.

As a rule, it is a man who sells the sugar-cane. The stalks stand in bundles behind him. When a customer comes, he cuts off a joint of the cane with a sharp knife. Mexicans are very fond of sugar-cane. Little boys and girls and even grown people sit along on the street curbings sucking and chewing it. All along the gutters are little tin stoves — some of them made of Mr. Rockefeller's oil-cans — on which the women cook tortillas and enchiladas for sale.

The baskets are incredibly cheap. I saw one so big that it looked as though it might have been one of the baskets in which Ali Baba hid the forty thieves. I asked the price, and the woman looked at me doubtfully as

THE PLAZA OF TEPIC

though she feared she were going to stun me with the figure. 'Dos pesos, Señor,' she said. One dollar! It must have cost some peasant woman in the mountains days and days of hard work to make that basket.

The quick, artistic eyes and the patient hands of these peasants have rescued many things from the rubbish-heaps. They use pieces of old automobile tires to make soles for their sandals. They make better guarachas than cowhide. Old burned-out electric-light globes are used in a quaint way. I have one in which a doll-like figure of the Virgin Mary is inside the globe, almost filling up the space. I can't imagine how the artist ever got the figure inside the globe. The figure is elaborate and beautiful. The Virgin wears a white dress with a yellow cloak thrown around her shoulders. On the front of the white dress is a large scarlet cross. At the foot of the figure is a cluster of palm sprays, and between the sprays, rising from the feet of the figure, are two tall poppies – one scarlet and one golden — all in wax. It is a delicate and charming little work of art which required artistry and endless intricate toil. Yet the woman asked only twenty-five cents of our money. The struggle for life and food is pitiful in Mexico.

Until I saw these markets at Tepic, I had supposed that Mexican sombreros were all alike. But I learned that almost every section of Mexico has its own pattern in hats. Those in Nayarit (of which Tepic is the capital) have little squashed-in tops, instead of the high peaks we see on all sombreros in pictures. Also the straw in these Tepic sombreros is so hard that the hats are all like iron. You could knock a man flat by hitting him with one. I don't see how they stand wearing them. They weigh like a cartload of bricks.

Everything in the costume of the peon has a reason. His sombrero has a brim that curls up at the edge because he has no pockets in his clothes and carries his treasures on his hat. His charro pants are of leather and very tight because he has to ride through brush. Now the charro costume continues as an expression of rural elegance. The jacket of the charro costume is short to give the hand a chance to travel quickly to the sash, and the sash is a memory of the Spanish sword-belt. High heels of the vaquero boots are not an affectation, but were made that way to keep the feet from slipping too far into the stirrups.

On special days, other peons come to the markets with ancient curios that they offer for sale, spread out on the sidewalks — old swords, ancient rusted daggers, spurs. Some have been dug out of the ground and plainly date back to the knights of the Conquest. Some of these swords were once proud weapons made in Toledo; have been stained with blood, and now end their story on a sidewalk next to a tamale peddler. The peons usually stay Saturday and Sunday. Then they start back to the hills again.

Everything in Tepic has the charm of great age. We went to see the manager of a cotton-mill and found his office had been an old Spanish inn with a cobblestone courtyard — great wide balconies and worn old stairways — queer dark passageways.

The hotel where we stopped had a grand name — Bola de Oro, the 'Ball of Gold.' It has no room telephones. When you want something, you walk out to the rail of the balcony and clap your hands. Some miracle seems to tell the world whether you want the little señora who does your room and your laundry, or the shine-boy who puts a gleam on your field boots, or the mozo who carries your trunk on his back, or the bathroom mozo. They all give you the impression that you are the lord of the manor and that they live only to make you happy.

Taking a bath at the hotel is no light and frivolous matter. You clap your hands for the mozo and he disappears into a distant part of the house and starts a wood fire under a tank. In due time, you start on a journey for a couple of miles through the house. It seems all right to wander around dressed about as Lady Godiva: Mexicans are not fussy. The bathtub is tin and the bathtowels are about the size of a lady's pocket handkerchief; but anyhow, it's a bath.

The people of Tepic are charming and friendly. One night, El Norteño and I were walking along a dark, narrow street and I was attracted by the sound of music coming from a little hotel. We walked in to see what was going on. As usual, in Mexican hotels, the dining-room was a sort of porch fronting on the patio. At a long table, a party of gay, jolly young fellows were giving a bachelor dinner to one who was about to be married. They were employees of a cigarette factory. Seeing us standing at the edge of the patio, looking on, one of the young fellows came over to ask if the Señor Gringo would not honor them by joining the party.

I spent all the rest of the evening with them. They were lovable, merry-hearted boys, and I had a grand time. They asked me what I would like to have the orchestra (two guitars and a violin) play. I asked first for *Rancho Grande*. They all stood up and roared its rollicking measures at the tops of their voices. Then I asked for *Cuatro Milpas*. I noticed that they all seemed pleased, but I

didn't know why. Then the toastmaster stood up and
thanked me for a charming compliment. I didn't understand how I had given them a charming compliment until
El Norteño whispered to me that those two tunes were
written on the heart of Tepic. Both were composed by
young men of Tepic and they were almost like national
airs.

The bridegroom was an official of the cigarette factory
and most of the guests worked there with him. We
toasted the bride with sentiment, romance, and poetic
license, for naturally she did not appear. With our limited
Spanish and their no-English-at-all, we did not understand their speeches and they did not understand ours —
which were frequent. I found this to be a distinct improve-
ment on listening to after-dinner speeches that you do
understand.

Coming home to the hotel, we encountered three very
dignified gentlemen who were walking down the middle
of the street arm in arm. Ahead of them was an orchestra
which they had hired to let the world know how they felt.
Occasionally they let out a defiant yell in concert: then
relapsed into majestic dignity again. In Mexico — especially here on the West Coast — I have seen often one
solitary Mexican walking all over town in grandeur in the
wake of an orchestra sounding the pæans of his triumph.
This is a magnificent crescendo of our American mood
of 'Drunk and glad of it.' Incidentally, there is very
little drunkenness in Mexico. The gentlemen who throw
eggs at the paintings in the bar-rooms are of another and
neighboring race.

When we got back to the hotel, we found a tense, excited conference going on. The center of the conference

was an elderly German banker, owner of vast Mexican properties. He was of such honor and integrity that he was trusted even by the bandits. This conference had to do with the bandits who had kidnapped the American mining-man. A rough-looking horseman had ridden in from the hills with a message written on a dirty piece of paper. The German banker handed it to me without comment. This is what it said:

'A menos que este mensajero vuelva mañana por la mañana, trayendo consigo treinta mil pesos, el Señor Bristow sera pasado por las armas al mediodia en punto.' (Unless this messenger returns to us safely tomorrow morning, bringing with him thirty thousand pesos, Mr. Bristow will be shot at the hour of noon.)

The German banker had wired to the relatives of Mr. Bristow; they were waiting in anxiety at Mazatlan. The messenger sat on his horse outside the hotel, waiting to gallop for the hills. Two cavalry officers were arguing with the German banker. They were urging him to ignore the message and let them start with the troops in pursuit. They were furious at the idea of temporizing with a bandit.

'But they would see you coming,' interposed El Norteño, butting into the conversation. 'And the Gringo gentleman would be killed.'

The cavalry officers flushed with anger at the interruption from a peon boy; but the old German banker looked at him reflectively and nodded gravely.

'We shall wait for a little while,' he said.

CHAPTER XIV
WHERE THE WEST BEGAN

THE beautiful Ramona was not impressed by the memories of Coronado. She lives in the old city of Compostela, from which Coronado started one January day in 1540 on his quest for the Seven Golden Cities of Cibola. The only thing that seemed to interest Ramona very much was to show me that she could play Yo-Yo (the game that we call Diablo) better than I. Between twirling the foolish spools on a string, I asked her if she did not often dream of Coronado.

'Coronado,' she said, trying to remember somebody named Coronado. 'Coronado — Coronado — Coronado ... Que es su nombre?'

'El Señor Francisco Vasquez Coronado.'

Ramona called back into the kitchen where her mother was making some enchiladas for our lunch. 'Mamacita, conoces un tal Francisco Vasquez Coronado?' (Little Mama, do you know a man named Francisco Vasquez Coronado?)

Mamacita said she did not know any such person, so Ramona turned back to Yo-Yo.

Ramona is about seventeen, with eyes that light up like hidden fires. Her mother runs a little store where she sells the worst enchiladas I ever tasted, pottery from Guadalajara, mule harness, and bottled beer. Ramona loves to dance, but there is no one with whom she can dance. She loves life, but the pigs in the street, the sleepy burro trains, and Mass at the old cathedral are all the excitement she can find.

Compostela drowses in its memories. It is perhaps the deadest town on the West Coast. All day long, old peons wrapped in scarlet serapes sit around in the little deserted plaza with dreams of other days in their black eyes. A young poet of my acquaintance — Donald Carr — wrote some charming verses about these old men in the park at Compostela.

> Ay, hombrecito de los viejos,
> Que sueño tiene en los negros ojos?
> Ay, pudieramos tambien quedar
> Soñando sueños por un avatar!
>
> POR DON CARR

> Oh, little old man,
> What dreams are in your black eyes?
> Oh, would that we could hold our dreams
> Throughout our lives!

I went to pay a visit to the old cathedral. It is a magnificent church and one of the historic shrines of our country, although we have forgotten it. The church was built in 1536, almost a hundred years before our Pilgrim Fathers landed at Plymouth Rock. After Coronado sallied out from Compostela in his long search for Cibola and its golden cities, Compostela became the capital from which all of the discovered lands were governed. So it is only truth to say that Compostela was the first capital of the land that was to be the United States. From this sleepy old town there went forth edicts and orders carried by couriers and messengers up through the lonely jungles, on through the mountain passes, through the country of the hostile Indians.

At one time there was a government palace — a palacio and a fortress for the soldiers. But it has been so completely ruined and effaced by Time that we could not be sure even of its location. The grandeur of Compostela did not last long. The bishop who founded the church, as the then farthest outpost of the Cross, never saw the church. He died before it was finished. The bishop who took his place died shortly after taking up his residence in Compostela. The third bishop was bored to tears by life in the sleepy, crude little garrison town and moved the seat of his authority to Guadalajara.

I have seen the old cathedral many times, but I never see it as it stands. To me it is always peopled by ghosts. I always see a cavalcade of Spanish soldiers in the street, their rough barb war-horses pawing and champing at the big bits; men-at-arms in their leather armor made of seven thicknesses of deerskin, with their huge bell-muzzled muskets, their lances and their great swords; the pack-horses and mules, with the muleteers endlessly tightening the cinch straps and rearranging the packs; the half-naked Indian allies looking on in wonderment; the chargers of the knights in armor held by the servants. And always from the dim recesses of the cathedral the solemn chants of the last Mass. And presently, in my mind's eye, I see the great studded front door swing open and the knights come stumping out in their armor to their horses. One horse is more splendid than the others, a long, sweeping saddle-cloth of gold and scarlet falling almost to his nervous, stamping hoofs — Coronado's war-horse.

At the head of the company of knights strides a handsome young man in armor — Coronado. History tells us that he was a gay young society blade of a powerful and influential family. When he started on this romantic quest, most of the knights who went with him were careless young aristocrats, out for a lark. Malicious gossip, perhaps, but tradition says that they threw away most of their armor the first day out because it got too heavy. In the first fight at Zuñi, two of the horsemen are said to have been so panic-stricken they put their saddles on hindside to. But in their breasts beat brave fighting hearts. Many a time when Coronado wanted to turn back, they insisted on keeping on in the face of danger, hunger, suffering, and fatigue. Coronado's instructions from the Viceroy were specific. When he found the Seven Golden Cities of Cibola, he was to load up two wagons with gold. The Viceroy decided to be modest; just two wagonloads of gold would be enough.

The old church hasn't changed much in all these years. Someone who wanted to show his gratitude and piety has put up a hideous clock-tower of bright blue on the front; otherwise it is as Coronado saw it.

The first time I saw the cathedral was during the period when the priests were in exile from Mexico and the Mexicans were holding services of their own. It was some kind of day of celebration. An old woman was leading the chants and litanies in a high, strident voice and the others joined in. All the women were on their knees on the cold stones. Some of them had come in from miles out in the country — on their knees every step of the way. As they came into the church, they prayed; then crawled a few inches nearer on their knees toward the altar. Near the altar was a group of young girls with crowns of thorns pressed down upon their foreheads. At one side was a large glass coffin in which there was a wax figure of

Jesus Christ, His body bloody and torn as it came from the Cross.

At the rear of the church was a middle-aged peon in white cotton drawers and shirt who was showing his little son how to tell the beads of his rosary as he prayed. At the end of the lesson, the child bowed respectfully and kissed his father's hand. For a moment it puzzled me; then I understood. It was a custom reaching back to days of chivalry. He was kissing the sword-hilt of the ruler of his House.

When I returned to California, I asked Mr. Ramon Novarro, the Mexican movie actor, about it. He was surprised that I should have been surprised. 'Why, certainly,' he said. 'I have never left my house in my life without kissing my father's hand.'

On the outside of the church is a cross carved into the stone. It stands at the height of a man's heart. All around the cross the stone is pock-marked by little holes. You know what that signified: bullets. No one knows how many men have been executed standing in front of that cross.

As we left the old church and walked through the sleepy streets of the adobe town, there came to our ears a queer, squealing noise, punctuated by the beat-beat-beat of a tom-tom. We started to investigate.

In an adobe house we found an impressive sight. The town butcher had got himself all-dressed-up in his best sombrero and his tightest leather pants. He had ridden his horse right into the house and was sitting in the saddle, trying to look like Napoleon at the battle of Austerlitz, or something. As he sat in silent grandeur, two little Indians played in his honor. One had a native pipe that looked something like a crude piccolo; the other had a tom-tom.

A curious custom all through this part of Mexico is to hire bands to play in one's honor. If you have done something of which you feel very proud or have a birthday or something, you hire a band and have it follow you around the streets tooting tunes by way of hurrahs.

I don't know what the town butcher had done that he was so proud of, but he had been sitting there for a long time on his horse like a statue, his face pulled into a very haughty and proud expression. When he saw us, he beckoned us to come in. There was a long and excited conversation between the Indian musicians, which we could not understand, as it was in some native dialect. Then the one who played the flute stood up and bowed and said, 'We will now play in honor of the Gringos. We shall play the national anthem of their great country — the United States.'

And then they solemnly proceeded to play what they thought was our national anthem.

It was 'Oh, Katarina'!

CHAPTER XV
BANDITS AND BULLS

ALL the next day we rode through a country filled with romance. This is the country of the charcoal-burners. We passed an old burned-out volcano about equally well known for charcoal and bandits. All over the mountainside we saw the huts and the furnaces of the charcoal-burners. At the railroad stations we saw charcoal heaped mountain high. They make it by burning the sap and green out of the fresh-cut boughs. Most of it goes to various parts of Mexico and to San Francisco, where many chefs still cook in the old style.

For almost half a day we rode through the ancient hacienda called San José de Condé. It dates back to 1550 and is one of the oldest farms in the New World. It is a little kingdom of itself with villages and great ranch-houses and outpost villages where the vaqueros live. At the main ranchhouse is a large town occupied by the ranch peons and an old church.

For generations the business of the San José de Condé has been raising bulls for bull-fights. They are not like the cattle we know. They are little black fellows as savage as tigers. Just as we breed cows for milk by picking out good milkers for mothers, so they breed bulls for fighting by killing off every calf that does not seem to hate men. The young ranch foreman told me that the fighting bulls are as savage and dangerous as any known wild animal. He told me of an instance where a bull chased a vaquero up a tree and kept him there for five days and nights, pawing the ground under the tree by way of challenge, only moving away for quick snatches of grass, literally sleeping with one eye on the tree. He said that the old ranch was going to abandon the business. Bulls for the fights do not pay. It is too risky. The fiercest bull may not pan out as a fighter once he is in the ring. If he doesn't, the fickle crowd begins to shout scorn and derision. The owners of the ranch are going to stock it with modern beef cattle.

There is a narrow strip of country near this old hacienda which is noted for scorpions. These venomous little insects always suggest a tiny leprous lobster to me. They have a deadly poison which is usually fatal to children. I know a woman who, stepping out of bed in the night in an old hotel, was stung by one. She said that it had the unusual effect of causing a partial paralysis of the motor nerves, yet an acute and agonizing sensitiveness of the skin. There is one hill near this place which the Government has fenced in, forbidding anyone to go there.

Late in the afternoon we passed through a tiny village on a lonely mountain road. There is a tradition that, in the old Spanish days, a company of soldiers deserted the colors and turned bandit. One of them — who was the chief bully — established a sort of robber kingdom back in the mountains, with bandits working for him on a payroll like cowboys. Descendants of those robbers — according to tradition — settled in this mountain village, every inhabitant a freebooter. If so, the inhabitants must in the meanwhile have experienced religion. With night coming on, we approached the place nervously. The women came out to meet us, bringing us presents of melons and fruit. One of the cars needed water and one of the peon women lugged it out by the gallon in an earthen jar, smilingly refusing pay for her work.

We arrived at the little town of Ixtlan at dark and found the sorry last chapter of a real bandit story. The German banker in Tepic — to the huge disgust of the army officers — had made a bargain with the bandits; they had reduced their demands from thirty thousand pesos to six thousand. That morning a messenger had gone out with a pack-horse loaded with silver money in linen sacks. The bandits had agreed to deliver Mr. Bristow at Ixtlan late that day. They wouldn't take a chance by bringing him to Tepic; and they warned the German banker that they would kill Bristow if any hostile movement was made by the troops.

We waited with considerable excitement, but Bristow did not come for a long time. Late that night, after the moon had risen, an elderly man rode into town, swaying from sickness and exhaustion, on a wretched old wreck of a cow-pony. It was Bristow. He found a place to stay and went to bed. When he had had time to rest a little, we went to the house to hear the story of his adventures.

As he told the story, he had been captured by four men. They had suddenly appeared out of the underbrush and leveled rifles at his head. They told his guide to go on his way and made Bristow ride with them. He said that he had no idea where they took him. He could speak only a few words of Spanish and they could speak no English, so all their conversation was carried on by signs. They took what money he had. One of the bandits took off his high field boots, which are considered a great prize in Mexico, and gave him a pair of sandals. One of them took his watch; another his gun; and they divided up his money which amounted to several hundred pesos.

For about twenty days he lived the life of a hunted coyote. The bandits were afraid of the troops. They were constantly on the move. Night and day they rode. They would ride into the mountains; suddenly double on their tracks, and strike off in a new direction. They were all mountain men and experienced riders, so they didn't mind the terrific pace and the fatigue. It nearly killed Bristow, who was an old man and in poor health.

From time to time a messenger would appear and there would be a conference. Then the messenger would ride away again. Bristow understood they were bargaining for his life. They made him perfectly well understand that, if the money did not arrive at a certain day, he would be killed. Otherwise than that, they were very good to him. He said when they got any food, they always gave him the best of it. When they killed a chicken, they gave him the choicest bits and ate the neck themselves. Sometimes they went without food altogether and gave what little they had to him. Whether this was really kindness, however, or merely the principle of feeding up a turkey for Thanksgiving Day, I do not know; and he didn't either.

When the messenger finally came back with the money, they rode with him some distance toward the nearest town; then they all fell back and disappeared except one. He went on with Bristow until the lights of the town could be seen in the distance. He carefully explained to the sick, tired old man how to find the rest of the road and vanished like a ghost into the night.

There was a garrison of Mexican troops in the town of Ixtlan. They were furious that the bandits should have been allowed to get away with this impudence. They were literally champing at the bits to take the trail against them. They insisted — and it was probably true — that, if they had had their way, there would have been no ransom; only dead bandits. Out of courtesy for the Gringo, they reluctantly stood apart and let the ransom be paid. But then — but then — the next chapter was theirs.

One of the officers drew for me a map in red, blue, and black ink by which he showed that they had every avenue of escape cut off for the bandits. To allow Bristow to come safely back to civilization, they had opened a place in the line, like a gate. Now they were going to close the gate. All through the night we heard the clatter of galloping horses as the cavalry patrols started for the hills. It was a mission of vengeance — to avenge their hurt pride.

We heard very little about it from the officials, but during the weeks that followed, the Mexican papers farther to the south where we had continued our journey published, now and then, small items stating that Jose Gomez — or somebody — a bandit had been caught and executed by the troops in the mountains of Nayarit. And I imagine that many a little pool of drying blood marked the spot where some bandit who had divided his chicken with the Gringo came to the end of his career. Some of them were, perhaps, surrounded and killed by troops. In many other cases, innocent-looking burro trains driven by peons and loaded with sugar-cane turned out to be moving forts — the sugar-cane hid machine guns.

Bristow said that when he was with the bandits they were almost starving. Most of the time a little corn meal mixed with water was all they could find to eat. One can imagine the torture of their fear after that, the leader

knowing that any member of his bandit band was likely
to turn traitor at any moment and kill him for the price
on his head: every peon passing with a burro likely to be
a soldier in disguise. Days and nights of terror — a
remorseless, bloodthirsty, untiring man hunt. The whole
incident was a grand thrill, but convinced me that the
life of a criminal is more unhappy and less profitable in
Mexico than elsewhere.

Wherever cussedness is abroad, you can usually find a
renegade American. According to rumor the real head of
the Ixtlan bandits is an American who lives a life of appar-
ent innocence in the town. There are reasons why he cannot go home to the 'States.'

Ixtlan is an old Aztec town. From the earliest times it
has been a stopping-place for travelers and an outpost for
troops — Aztec, then Spanish, now Mexican. We were
the only guests at a little country inn. It was a sort of
family affair. They tried hard to make us happy. The
head of the household was a widow; we seldom saw the
señora, although she came in every morning to wish us
good-morning and every night to wish us pleasant dreams.

The two daughters of the household waited on the table
and made the beds in the old high-ceilinged bedrooms.
The eldest was Amparo. She was pale and lithe with
eyes in which dreams slumbered. She was very much dis-
tressed if we didn't eat everything, which was quite impossible because she brought it on by armloads. In the
evening, she played the phonograph, and as she put on
each new piece looked around anxiously to ask, 'Le gusta?'
(You like it?)

The other daughter was Juanita. She had eyes that lit
up suddenly with humor. But her delicate mouth was sad

and turned down at the corners. Her face was strong with
Spanish strength. In the face of Amparo was the sugges-
tion of the beauty of another race — probably Toltec or
Aztec. But Juanita was proud and Spanish.

Amparo was something of a coquette. One day she
invited one of the young engineers to go to Mass with her;
then told him she was going at 5 A.M.

In the evenings they played rummy for hours with the
engineers, not having an idea what it was all about.

A Mexican girl has but one thought — to do what her
men want. The domestic mores of the Eastern purdah
still hold her.

Her first social contact with American boys leaves her
dazed. Great social changes are being made in Mexico by
girls who have been educated in the United States.

After her marriage, the Mexican girl becomes the empress of her own household. All Mexican women of social
breeding and mature years impress me as being very much
alike. They cover their shyness with a regal dignity, but,
having let down the bars, are witty, animated, and with a
genius for intimacy. They are easily offended, however,
by the slightest breech of ceremonious etiquette. When an
opportunity comes, they often show high executive ability
— the product of their experience as chatelaines of great
households. If you are accepted into a Mexican household,
you find yourself overwhelmed with a tender maternal
anxiety for your happiness and welfare.

Maria was the maidservant — the criada. She did all
the laundry work and helped in the kitchen and pumped
the water into the funny old shower bath for us. Maria
was small and wistful. But she was pretty, too, in a
timid, shrinking way.

Pedro was the old manservant. He helped us with our baggage and eagerly ran our errands. In leaving, we gave him a tip. He looked at it and — although it seemed very little to us — ran down the street after us to give it back and ask for something smaller. He protested it was too much. If Pedro ever gets a job in an American hotel, the other bellboys will all insist that he be examined for insanity.

CHAPTER XVI
AN OLD AZTEC TOWN

It was Palm Sunday in Ixtlan. I was wakened that morning by a queer thumping sound on the pavement outside my window. A young Indian was on his way to church. As penance for his sins he was torturing himself. He had made a cross of timbers so enormous that the weight almost crushed him. He was crawling on his hands with the cross on his back. It was so heavy that he could only struggle along for a few feet at a time. He had been crawling all night, since sundown the day before, from his hut in the hills. His face was drawn and pale, for he had eaten nothing. His knees were bleeding from contact with the hard stones.

The church at Ixtlan is very, very old. The congregation is of almost pure Aztec descent and the church somehow takes on the strangeness of that vanished race. The old belfry tower was a fortress and its time-grayed sides are torn by bullet marks. It is the shrine of a wild fierce country.

The church was packed with peons whose Indian blood showed in their faces. Each one held in front of his face the frond of a palm as the priests passed down the aisles in the ceremonial procession. Ragged people, fierce people with wild eyes. In the hope of a miracle, the steps of the church were thronged with sick babies, some of whom were blind and some horribly deformed. Many were carried to the place by tiny little girls not much bigger than the babies themselves. Having deposited the babies, they sat and waited in hopeless, patient silence.

It was a great fête day as well as a day of religious celebration. The sidewalks were packed with peddlers and booths. Some sold beads of colored glass; others, religious medallions, tortillas, sticky cactus candy, sugar-cane. One peddler had a board spread with relics — odd spurs, garden tools, old knives with half the blades broken, daggers with rusted blades. In the midst of this trash was a court sword that had belonged to a Spanish knight.

When we pulled out of Ixtlan, that day, our automobiles bumped and thumped over the ruts of one of the oldest roads in the Western Hemisphere. It was the old Spanish treasure-road over which the long pack-mule trains carried the cargoes of the galleons from San Blas over the mountains to Vera Cruz. It was almost pitiful to think of the labor that had gone into the making of that road. The pavement was made of small cobblestones fitted together like a mosaic. In the days of the treasure-trains, it must have been like a modern bathroom floor. For centuries it has been allowed to go to rack and ruin. Deep cañons have been cut into it by the cloudburst waters that come surging down from the hills. In places it is as much as a loaded burro can do to pick his way around the gullies and barrancas in the road.

As we were fighting our way in low gear over this road, we met a burro train loaded with long planks that gave the effect of each little burrito carrying his stall along with him. One slipped and fell. With those long boards fastened to his sides, he could not get up again until some of our engineers climbed out of the cars, grabbed the ends of the boards, and lifted him back to his feet. The peon who drove the train must have been astonished, for no Gringo had ever shown any interest in him before, but his face was absolutely impassive as he raised his big sombrero and murmured, 'Muchas gracias, señores.'

The road finally got so bad that we decided to tear down a piece of the stone wall that lined the road, first having asked permission of the Presidente — of whom, more later on. A surprise met us in that wall. For hundreds of miles these walls line the road and crawl over the hills until your eye loses them in the distance. We thought we could toss down the stones as in a New England stone wall. When we tried it, we found that every stone was wedged and fitted in so carefully that we had to pry it out with automobile tools. No wonder those walls have stood there since the days of Cortez! Everywhere in Mexico you have to be impressed with the superb engineering genius of those old Spanish Conquistadores. It may be they were cruel and tyrannical and greedy in their hunt for gold, but they had brains.

We found El Norteño waiting for us at a camp that some of our party had established at a place called Porto Suelo. The boys had pitched their tents right in the middle of the old treasure-road. It was the first time we had taken the tents from the baggage trucks, and we all thought it was a good deal of fun. The tents were little tan-colored houses with one pole in the middle like a Sioux Indian tepee. At the front of the tent, part of the wall let down to make a little window, protected from insects by wire netting. Each of us had an army cot and a canvas sleeping-bag, lined with blanketing. To Norteño's huge delight, the sleeping-bags could be opened and closed with zippers.

We set up a long folding camp-table at one side of the

road and got out the kitchen equipment. There was a camp stove with a gasoline flame. El Norteño was very much astonished as he came into camp, struggling with a huge armload of wood, to learn that we had a machine that talked like a man — our camp phonograph. He helped us to set up another mysterious instrument which had a long jointed pole that was braced against the winds of the tropic night by guide-wires tied into the stone walls of the time of Cortez. El Norteño had never heard of a radio outfit, and the operator let him wear the head-piece and hear the faint little buzzing clicks. He looked politely skeptical, however, when he was told that those little clicks were coming from a boy in a little town in Ohio who had caught them by accident as he was feeling around in the air waves. Another one was coming from a sleepy army operator in Honolulu who suddenly came to life as he realized who was sputtering into the air, and who courteously agreed to take the message from the Mexican mountains and relay it for us back to Los Angeles.

Our camp was right in the middle of the 'main-traveled' road up from the mysterious Barranca country to Ixtlan and the big towns beyond. All day long and far into the night, the burro trains pattered through our camp between the cook-tent and our sleeping-tents. It was a procession I shall never forget. Some of the burros were loaded with jars and pots to be sold in the markets of Tepic. Some had crates of chickens or turkeys and several had squealing pigs. Some were serving as carriages, carrying women and children. All the women were riding sideways — sometimes curled around Mexican cow-saddles and sometimes on blankets. From one end of Mexico to the other, I have never seen but one woman riding what we call astraddle. She was the beautiful young wife of an army officer with a haughty, cold face. She was fashionably dressed in white duck with a gorgeous gold-embroidered sombrero. When her wild young thoroughbred shied at our cars, she lashed him with merciless cuts of a gold-mounted quirt — without a trace of expression on her 'poker face.'

Late at night one little family came through the camp with two sleepy babies in panniers on the sides of a burro and a timid little mother plodding alongside. We always marveled at the wonderful way in which these loads were packed on the saddles. Just try, for the benefit of your soul, fastening a pack on a burro's back. The darn thing slides one side, then the other side. It usually winds up its career under the burro's stomach. Try then to pack a burro with fragile, jiggly native pottery, and you will come to the conclusion that the most famous of our diamond-hitch experts of the old border days still had something to learn from a Mexican mule-driver. The driver urged the little beasts on by shouting 'Aye–bur–r–o'!

What impressed us was the perfect courtesy of these simple little peons. You can imagine what must have been their secret astonishment to come suddenly upon this camp of strange Gringo gentlemen with queer tents, high radio poles, and the sputtering flash of the radio itself. All day and far into the night they came, but of all that procession I did not see one who stared. They lifted their sombreros, murmured 'Buenos noches, señores,' but looked neither to the right nor to the left. I cannot claim that we were equally courteous.

Many features of our camp fascinated El Norteño. Especially the patent can-opener. To tell the truth, I was fascinated myself by the can-opener. To his ineffable bliss, he was allowed to lift the lid from the cans, and had we not been firm, he would have gone on de-lidding all the cans on the West Coast of Mexico. The coffee percolator came next of rank in his wonderment. After that my typewriter. He would plant himself in front of that instrument, watching the quick clicking keys with entrancement. Only the coffee percolator could wean away his attention. He liked to watch that bubble. So also did we. It was an oasis in a desert.

My frank admiration for Mexico stops just this side of the coffee. To our taste, at least, it is terrible. They do not grind the berries as we do. They pulverize them until they become a brown talcum powder. This they boil until it is like lye. Very often they bring the coffee around cold in a pitcher, and pour a portion into your cup. To this they add either hot water or hot milk, as your sins deserve. Whenever I took hot milk, I was sorry I had not asked for hot water, and when I chose hot water, my regret was agonizing that I had not asked for milk. It is pretty awful either way. To the Mexican palate, ours is just as bad. In some of the larger Mexican cities they ask you if you would like to have café americano. Say 'Yes'! Say 'Sí'! Yell it! Don't let there be any mistake.

From Ixtlan there had come with us as a guard of honor a troop of cavalry — the bodyguard and escort of El Presidente, the boss of the town. He was a gorgeous figure. He was enormously fat, but he rode like a centaur. His mount was a dun-colored mule. His saddle was a thing of mystic beauty. It was mounted in solid gold. His bridle was fit for a prince of Cathay. All his personal clothes, from his sombrero heavy with silver embroidery to his enormous silver spurs, went with the outfit. Leaving us in camp with the soldiers, El Presidente took two of our engineers and two mounted scouts and went away to find if possible a road over which our automobiles could travel.

We were interested in our troopers. They were so quiet. All day long they sat on the high land above with their carbines across their knees, saying scarcely a word. Once in a while they played a Mexican card-game. Three times a day they cooked their tortillas. They accepted our canned goods with shy thanks, but I don't think they liked the stuff much. One of our party was a Mexican navy officer, sent with us as an honorary escort. He was a charming and interesting fellow. Once during the afternoon he borrowed a carbine from a soldier and we had a target contest: but the fouled, worn-out cavalry weapon was a poor second against our American repeating rifles. Their horses were a poor lot. They explained that the good horses disappeared in the havoc of the last revolution. The soldiers themselves, however, were fine military material. I doubt if there is another soldier in the world who will march so far or fight so courageously or uncomplainingly on a diet of corn cakes which he cooks himself.

One of the party had a movie camera. To relieve the boredom, a young army major, who had joined our party at Tepic, suggested that we stage a play about bandits. He stopped the next man who came along on a burro and explained to him that he had been cast for the part of the bandit. He was a handsome young fellow and played the part like a movie hero. When the major suggested that the soldiers hang him by the neck as a fitting finale to the drama, we made hasty objections. 'But we could cut him down before he really choked,' said the major. The peon did not offer the slightest objection. He apparently thought it would be a grand idea and great realism. He was the one most obviously disappointed when we declared the drama ended with the hero still unhanged.

That night was the most gorgeous moonlight night I ever remember to have seen. The mysterious shadow of the mountain fell caressingly across a fairyland sunk in a deep cañon. The Mexican major and I walked out along the old treasure-road. He talked of the relations between the United States and Mexico. Without a close understanding friendship between the two countries, Mexico will be a Belgium for any European country seeking to invade the United States, a fatal vantage-ground from which it will be possible to strike at the heart of America. The talk then turned to art and music. He was speaking of an orchestra leader in the City of Mexico who has a new and interesting interpretation of Mendelssohn. Suddenly he thrust out an arm and swept me around behind him, shielding my body with his. His heavy army revolver was out of the holster and in his hand as he tensely watched a movement in the shadow. The chaparral parted and a burro came through into the moonlight.

The major laughed. 'You never know,' he said. He put his revolver back into the holster. 'We were speaking of Mendelssohn.'

'Compañero,' I said, hoping he would not hear my knees shaking, 'compañero, excuse me but I cannot intelligently discuss Mendelssohn with gooseflesh trickling down my backbone. Let's go back and go to bed.'

CHAPTER XVII

THE BARRANCAS

IF YOU can imagine what it would be like, trying to drive a car down Bright Angel Trail and across Grand Cañon, you may get an idea what it was like when our engineers forced two small automobiles through the Barrancas.

This is one of the greatest gulches in the world. It is a giant gash in the heart of the high mountains near the border of Nayarit and the State of Jalisco. Until an American railroad company built a track hugging the face of the mountains that tower above the Barrancas, Guadalajara, the second city of Mexico, was a city cut off — marooned. Either you mounted a mule and plodded over mountains through a district at that time infested by bandits, or you made an enormous circuit by sea. The Southern Pacific Railroad tackled the terrific job of laying rails that encircled the rim of the great chasm. It is said to be the most difficult and expensive stretch of railroad construction in the Western Hemisphere — perhaps in the whole world. And now that it is built, it is one of the most amazing and beautiful train rides in the world. But it did not help motor traffic in any way. The problem of our party of engineers was to blaze a trail for automobiles.

Back in the days of the Conquest, the Spaniards built a road through the Barrancas: the San Blas to Vera Cruz treasure-road pitched down over the brink of the big cañon and crawled up the other side. With the passing of time, this road had gone to ruin. Whole sections of it had pitched down over the edge of precipices. What remained of it was cut into cañons. It was an impediment rather than a passage. There were places where a burro had to be packed very lightly, to stumble and crawl over. The nature of the ground may be assumed from the fact that one section of the Barrancas bears the appropriate name — Salsipueda (Get out if you can).

We sent two of the five cars back to Ixtlan to be shipped by flatcar to Magdalena on the side of the cañon. The remaining two cars which were to make the trip were stripped of their baggage load. A soldier had been sent ahead to arrange for ox-teams. A troop of cavalry rode behind to supply the man power.

The cars were scarcely outside of our roadside camp when the trail pitched down over the brink. It will always remain one of the epics of automobile driving. But it is not interesting to tell about. There were places where the cars had to hug burro trails on the perilous faces of mountain cliffs, the wheels held on the edge by ropes and soldiers. There were places where they had to go up hills that were like climbing the side of a sky-scraper. It was a matter of backing up for a start, then a mad plunge of a few feet in low gear, then another start. There were places where six oxen pulled with their might and main ahead, a troop of dismounted cavalry pushed from behind, while the engine roared and screamed. It is a tribute to modern automobile makers that not even a tire was punctured during this terrific ordeal.

At the bottom of the cañon is a lonely, desolate little Mexican town whose inhabitants would no doubt die of homesickness were they removed to a spot more favored. The gentleman who wrote 'Home, Sweet Home,' touched a mysterious phase of human character. At the end of the Apache wars, Geronimo and his renegade warriors were sent as prisoners to the most beautiful part of Florida. They yielded to the inevitable in the matter of losing their freedom, but some of them literally died of longing for the God-awful desolation of the burning Arizona deserts. One Apache chief explained the loneliness of his heart by saying, 'I can't look anywhere except up if I wish to see anything.' I don't know how the folks in Blandabarrancas explain their attachment.

From one brink to the other, the automobiles fought their way twenty-eight miles over a motor Purgatory. Having shipped myself with the cars from Ixtlan, I found them resting on cots in a wretched little hotel in the town of Magdalena. It is a tradition that the hero who came through Pickett's charge at Gettysburg usually shoots his arm off with a Fourth-of-July firecracker. Just so the only damage to any of our cars was in taking one of them off the flatcars at the unloading.

Magdalena was interesting, but did not tempt us to linger. There is a tradition that the mysterious hidden gold mine of the Aztec Emperor Montezuma was near Magdalena. More recent and more cold-blooded investigations of the stories of the Spanish Conquest bring a note of skepticism to these treasure tales. They considerably reduce Montezuma's financial rating in Bradstreet's. Historians are beginning to wonder if the Aztecs had much gold. Their interest seems to have turned to other minerals — obsidian, turquoise.

An ancient letter from a soldier of the Conquest has been found. In telling the news to the folks back home, he says that, when Cortez had to retreat from the city

THROUGH THE BARRANCAS BY AUTOMOBILE — WITH THE
HELP OF SOLDIERS AND OXEN

Tenochtitlan (the present Mexico City), an order gave
the soldiers the usual privileges of a forced retreat — the
privilege of looting. They could carry off all the gold they
could find. He writes with sardonic bitterness that he
wishes he had stayed at home in Spain and herded goats.
Whether or not Montezuma got his gold from Magdalena,
the fact remains that others have found gold there. Rich
and important mines have been, and are being, worked by
American and British interests.

What interested me in Magdalena was the old church.
It has a marvelous crucifix — a life-size figure of Christ
that is reputed to shed real blood at certain significant
periods. A book might be written of some of the sacred
figures found in Mexican churches. The artists of that
period were nothing if not literal. The figure of the Cross
is not conventionalized as in our modern artistry. Most
of them depict the last episode of a human being dying in
awful agony. It calls out the sympathy of the simple,
warm-hearted little peons — to them the Christ is their
intimate friend. The day we visited the old church, a little
Mexican boy of perhaps ten years was clinging to the
blood-stained, worn, fragile hand of the Christ, kissing
the hand again and again, murmuring caressing, loving
words of sympathy and consolation.

I found a volunteer guide in a smart Syrian from
Beyrout. He was clever, illuminating, and brazen. The
Syrians are all over Mexico. They are the sharp traders,
the money pioneers. This one told me shamelessly how
he had captured the trade of the town from the Mexican
merchants. He said the gag was to pretend great friendship — to play on the hearts of the peasants. 'I tell Mrs.
Lopez,' he said, 'that the fellow across the way would

charge her more: but to show her how warm my heart is for the people of Mexico, I am going to let her have her corn meal and pink dresses very cheap.'

Although this may be effective in the homeland, the Mexican is disillusioned by the time he gets to the United States. The patent-medicine shows of Arizona find the Mexican suckers hard-boiled and wary. My friend Slim Sheets, who sells the world's most marvelous corn cure between acts of the most wonderful vaudeville show on earth, tells me that a Mexican will never buy anything until after the third day. He waits to observe the experience of some Gringo friend before he is prepared to believe that an ointment rubbed on the outside of a shoe will cure the corn inside.

My Syrian friend said that another factor of his success lay in introducing into Magdalena the dollar-down-dollar-a-week system. Like every other transplanted Gringo whom I consulted, he said that the Mexican peon was good pay — a square shooter and commercially honorable.

We drove out late that afternoon through narrow little streets where the women sat in doorways nursing babies. We were in the mescal country now — hills covered with the fat-leaved maguey century plants that yield Mexico's national liquor. A Mexican maguey hacendado has a long wait ahead. Several years must elapse before the crop is ready to 'pick' — and then it is not picked. Mescal is made by cooking and fermenting the root which grows almost to the thickness of a man's body; the result is a yellowish-white liquid very intoxicating and of indescribable taste. Tequila is a refinement of mescal.

We stopped that night in what had been a lovely old suburban villa and had been turned into the worst hotel of my not inconsiderable experience. It was more suggestive of a Pompeian villa than a Mexican house — great square rooms looking out on loggias, patios following patios. The bedchambers were not alluring. The mattresses were of board. I drew a room with two engineers. At bedtime, one remarked with heavy sarcasm: 'We leave to you the choice. Do you prefer the oak bed or the spruce?' We were warned not to step around in the dark on account of scorpions.

In the midst of our misery, we found light. At breakfast next morning, we discovered ourselves sitting seatmate to one of the most interesting men in Mexico, a tiny, sprightly old man with long whiskers. It was Dr. Atl, the greatest expert in the world on Mexican churches. He has written a work in six volumes which is recognized as the last word. I thought it was strange that there should still be one in Mexico with a name so essentially Aztec. Then I learned that his private name is quite different. He comes from an old Spanish family. His heart from childhood was ever with the vanished Aztecs. Also it was an unfilled desire of his heart to be a doctor. Whereupon, returning from a long sea voyage, he announced to an astonished world that from that point on he was to be known as Dr. Atl, and from that point on began the real achievements of his life. He is also an artist, a painter of international fame, and a chemist of high repute.

The idea that anyone could write six huge volumes on the churches of Mexico so staggered me that I felt drawn into the impertinence of expressing my wonderment. 'But, after all,' I hastened to add apologetically, 'it must be a great satisfaction to realize that you have absolutely exhausted a subject.'

Dr. Atl looked as though he were going to faint with astonishment. 'Exhausted the subject!' he gasped. 'My dear fellow, I haven't even seen one third of the churches of Mexico.'

He told us much that was interesting as we ate breakfast, facts that were of value to travelers coming into one of the great centers of New World architecture — Guadalajara. What seem to us now as Old-World architecture — buildings that whisper of ancient days — were the product of an outburst of a glorious period when Youth found an outlet.

The myriad cathedrals and churches of Mexico represent a golden age of young untrammeled architecture. Working under the masters of architecture in Europe, there were a great number of young artists who champed at the bit. As with many brilliant boys bending over drawing-boards of today, they had to do what they were told. The Spanish Conquest — the opening of a new heathen, churchless land to the Cross and the throne — was their opportunity. Their artistic handcuffs suddenly knocked off, they could work out their own ideas. Never in the history of the world was there such an era of church building. In a period of about one hundred years, more than fifteen thousand important churches were built. An average of more than three a week! Not many of these stand as they were made. Many have been rebuilt several times. Just as in the case of the missions of California. I used to stand in their shadows and imagine myself standing with the good Father Junipero Serra until I discovered that Serra only saw one or two of the present missions. Many of them are not even on the spots that he built. The mission at Santa Barbara has been completely rebuilt four times.

I have spent a great part of my life admiring the voices that were off key, and standing transfixed with admiration in front of pictures that the committee was about to banish to the dark cellars: so, in a hoarse whisper of warning, I will pass on the verdicts of Dr. Atl. He says that the cathedral at Pueblo is by far the finest in Mexico. In Guadalajara the best architecture is to be found in the Santuaro and the church of San Felipe de Jesus. So now, if you go home, raving over the wrong church, don't blame me.

CHAPTER XVIII

A SPANISH CITY IN MEXICO

GUADALAJARA always goes straight to the heart of the visiting American. It is different in atmosphere and psychology from any other Mexican city. In essence it is Spanish rather than Mexican. It was established in 1530 — about a hundred years before the Pilgrim Fathers landed at Plymouth Rock — by Captain Juan de Oñate in honor of his commanding officer, Nuño de Guzman, who was born in Guadalajara, Spain.

It is fifty-two hundred feet above sea-level and I have an idea that its perfect, sparkling climate has something to do with its psychology. It is cynical, perverse, gay, attractive, sophisticated. Independent, 'contrary' — almost as we would say, in the slang of the day, 'snooty.' Mexican politicians say with some sourness that, whatever question arises, Guadalajara is always on the other side. Whoever you are, Guadalajara is not in the least impressed. No one escapes its gay, witty ridicule. The city has been fought over; bombarded, invaded times without number, but no tragedy can dim its spirits — as crisp and volatile as its mountain air. The air never gets hot and the Guadalajareños never get heated. It lies in the dip made by an extinct volcano, and its climate has an electrical exhilaration and tingle.

The city is gorgeous with churches. It is the real center of the Catholic Church in Mexico — a city of devotion underneath its cynicism. From my hotel windows I could count twenty-three magnificent churches. There are, I believe, some fifty in all, not counting the small ones.

The hotels are colorful and charming. I have stayed at several. All have a quaint foreign atmosphere. In each one the rooms open out onto a great balcony, which in turn looks down into a handsome rotunda. You never have the sense of being fodder for a factory as in so many American hotels. There is a feeling that they want you apart from your money. They have a real anxiety as to your happiness and peace of mind. The whole staff galloped up in a body when I announced that my bath would not run hot water. It developed that the native plumber — not being a linguist — had put the 'hot' sign on the cold faucet.

The first day I walked abroad in Guadalajara, I was stopped by a little boy about fourteen years old. He wanted to know if I wanted a guide. He said he was very poor and had four little brothers and sisters to support. As our intimacy continued from day to day, he kept increasing the number of brothers and sisters until I became alarmed lest he should turn out to be blood brother to all the half orphans in Mexico. The thing that reassured me in this regard was his nationality. He was not Mexican. His people had come from Indiana, his father being a miner as well as the champion father of all time in point of production. My little friend said he had been born in Guadalajara. We spent a pleasant and valuable morning together. He knew where we could find old Spanish chests, red and gold Chinese chests — a little cylindrical chest with one flat side that was for the back of a carriage. He did all the bargaining. He beat the dealers down in their prices; then excused himself to go back to

collect. When we marched back in triumph to the hotel
with our arms filled with bundles and two cargadores
following with the chests, the clerk at the desk almost
fell over in his tracks.

'Where did you get that boy?' he demanded. The boy
looked like innocence on a monument saddened by the
evils of the world. 'I found him on the street,' I said uneasily. 'He found you on the street,' retorted the clerk.
'And before he goes, you had better look to see if your
watch is still there. He is the most notorious pickpocket
in Guadalajara. He is just out for an airing before he goes
back to jail again.' I remembered that he had shown a
remarkable familiarity with the premises when we had
gone to look over the jail — a great courtyard surrounded
with cells from which the dejected inmates spoke pleas-
antly to my guide.

He was the first of many interesting acquaintances I
picked up on the streets. Another was Señorita Maria
Guadalupe Pecheco, with whom I had a desperate flirta-
tion. The señorita was of the age of five years. She sold
newspapers in front of the Imperial Hotel.

'Look at that child's burning eyes!' I exclaimed to
one of the engineers as we stopped to buy a paper from
her. 'Don't they scorch a way right into your heart?'
The señorita listened gravely and — as we thought —
without understanding. We asked her name, but she
turned bashfully away. The next morning at breakfast
I felt a little soft hand on my knee and I looked down to
see this lovely baby. In a little soft voice, watching my
face meanwhile, she said: 'Mi nombre es Maria Teresa
Pacheco, y yo tengo ojos calientes. Hagame el favor de
darme cinco centavos para un periodico.' (My name is

Maria Teresa Pacheco, and I have hot eyes. Do me a
favor; give me five cents for a paper.)   We gave Maria
Teresa many five-cent pieces until we observed to our
pain that, at intervals, an older woman came and took the
money away from her.

Guadalajara is famous for the beauty of its girls. They
are lovely beyond all description, but it will do you no
good to know about it. The old Spanish customs prevail.
It is unheard of for a girl to be on the street alone. To go
anywhere with a boy unchaperoned is unheard of and
unthinkable. The city was all torn up over the scandal
of some of the young married people bathing in Lake
Chapala with modern bathing-suits and — horrors of
horrors — men and women together. The debate reached
such proportions that the Archbishop was finally called
in. To the dismay of the older people, he smiled and said
he couldn't see any harm.

Love is complicated in Guadalajara. Either the smitten
young sheik goes to the father and asks for the hand of a
girl he has only seen at a distance or he 'plays bear' at
her window. This charming custom — hacer el oso — is
the last stand of the true romance on the American continent. Guadalajara is an old-fashioned city with narrow
streets and the houses are built out to the sidewalks
elbow to elbow without a space or an inch between.
Family life goes on in the secluded patios. But in front
there are heavily barred windows that look out upon the
street. The boys come to these windows and whisper
soft nothings to the girl sitting in darkness on the other
side of the bars. Every night you see scores of these sidewalk courtships. The girl sits on a window-seat and the
boy leans with a swagger against the wall outside. The

lovers seem completely oblivious to the throngs passing
on the sidewalks. Sometimes the families are complacent
and shut their eyes. Sometimes the swain stands at the
window and hears no response from within. He may not
call. He can only wait and champ up and down in front
of the window like a bear in a cage — waiting and wondering. There are girls whose reign as belles is so great that
pathways have been worn in the cement in front of their
windows. I have known of cases where a boy stood in
front of a girl's window for three years every night —
hoping and adoring. Once in a while he finally gets in;
usually he doesn't.

Among the houses of Guadalajara there are a few of a
somewhat later era that were built in two stories, somewhat on the order of the balcony houses of Monterey,
California. It distinctly cramps the style of the whispering lover to be obliged to murmur soft caresses from the
sidewalk to a second-story window. To meet this emergency, some bright, progressive young fellow introduced
the portable telephone as a messenger of true love. This
he managed to send to the girl. When the dusk of evening
came, she would softly pass down the end of the telephone
line and they would exchange their vows under the benign
influence of the late Alexander Bell. While we were in
Guadalajara a tragedy occurred. The palpitating swain
came along the street — burning with romantic ardor —
to discover another swain whispering soft nothings to his
lady-love over the telephone which she had treacherously
lowered to him. The interloper finished his song of love
in the morgue.

A touch of Mexican city life that never fails to interest
Americans is in the cargadores. Hordes of them hang

around the railroad depots — they are the Red Caps and
the express wagons of Mexico. They grab your suitcases
and your trunks and trot off as though they had a load
of feathers. I have seen two cargadores carrying a grand
piano through the streets on their backs. Their strength
is all in their legs. I have seen these human pack-horses
fail to lift a bundle of moderate weight. But once get the
weight shifted to their shoulders and their power is simply
incredible. A heavy trunk that would cause two of our
baggage-smashers to groan and complain — simply rolling
it along a platform — is as nothing to a cargador. If
there are any express wagons in Mexico, I have never
seen any. When you buy the usual loot at the antique
stores, the proprietor calls a cargador or two cargadores
and they go trotting off to the hotel or depot with heavy
boxes packed for shipment on their shoulders.

If you are intending to do much shopping in Guadalajara, it is not unusual to call a cargador to carry
your money. There is gold to be had, but the usual
medium of exchange is the silver peso, valued at from
forty-five to fifty cents according to the rate of exchange.
To wander around on a shopping excursion with what
amounts to two or three hundred dollars in silver half-
dollar pieces is no light job. At the bank they give you
small linen sacks with the money and you walk, lugging
these sacks in your hands. It is not unusual to see a cargador from a bank walking along the streets with a back-
load of money. No one thinks of a guard. This is probably due in part to the intrinsic honesty of the Mexican;
due in part to the embarrassment that would confront a
robber finding himself with a wheelbarrow filled with
money to trundle along in his flight. I have often seen a

peon wheeling a barrow filled with money along the sidewalk.

Shopping in Guadalajara is a quaint and interesting experience. One of the best places to buy old chests is in an open patio behind the Governor's palace, where an old man has collected them from places that he alone knows. If you are not careful, however, in his beaming anxiety to please he will 'fix them up' by painting the horsehide lids with black paint and putting in new brass nails. There is another curio store in an old house on a side street. There are two or three stories of space loaded with junk, among which are priceless things. The proprietor is a charming old man with an amiable indifference as to whether or not you buy. If you don't like what he has there, he can be persuaded to open up two other houses where he has other treasures stored. He has no clerks, and 'salesmanship' is something of which he has never heard. I think, on the whole, he rather hates to part from anything in his collection.

There are two public markets where the Mexican Indians sit in silence — in inscrutable passivity — while you look at their sugar-cane stalks, their blankets, their pottery, their dulces, their guarachas. There is here none of the cocky indifference you sometimes encounter in tradesmen; no 'independence' of spirit. It is an attitude of complete acceptance of fate. If you wish to buy, that is your affair. Why should they tell you whether or not you should buy?

One of these public markets is in the heart of the business district. The other is in the lower part of town in a great square in front of a municipal building. In latter years, the municipal government has built regular stalls

for some of the little sidewalk merchants where trade
goes on much as in our markets. But the Indians who sit
outside in the gutters and on the ground go on in the old
way. Going to market is a social event with them. They
sit in the nest of their flounce of calico skirts — seeing
nothing, yet seeing everything — until their packload of
sugar-cane is gone; then they go back to the mountains,
the delectable vacation having ended. Booths and glass
counters would spoil their one great entertainment.

Around the great plaza in Guadalajara is an arcade that
runs in front of the buildings. This is called the Portales.
It is an alluring place. Serapes hang from the pillars of
the arcade. Dulce counters crowd booths where machetes
are sold. Sacred images next to guarachas. It all has the
gay air of a country fair. Behind these arcades are the
regular department stores. Most of them are run by
French people. In Mexico the nationalities fall into places
established by race characteristics. The stores that appeal
to women are mainly French. The factories and many of
the banks are in the hands of Germans. The public
utilities — such as gasoline, street railroads, etc., requiring
large outlays of capital — are likely to be under the
management of Americans or Canadians.

Of these foreigners, the Germans have been the most
successful with the Mexicans. Young German boys of
good families and efficient education come from the
Fatherland and marry into Mexican families. They learn
the language thoroughly and the customs of the people.
Such marriages are almost invariably happy. The French
keep strictly to themselves. They have their own clubs
and their own social circles. Usually they are working
toward the day when they can retire and go home to

Paris. The Americans are of various types. Mexico is filled with young college men of charming manners and high attainments who have gained respect and liking in Mexico — and by 'slickers' who find it convenient to stay on the far side of the international line. A visitor to Mexico — meeting other Americans — is filled either with pride or shame; seldom by halfway emotions. One thing that brings great discredit and contempt for American tourists is the way the men sometimes drink. They suggest nothing so much as a locomotive stopping at a desert water-tank.

American women who go to live in Mexico are seldom completely happy while they are there and are never happy after they leave. There is something in the gay, careless leisure that, once experienced, can never be forgotten. Most American women, going with their young husbands to Mexico, get a thrill out of the unaccustomed luxury of so many quiet servants — a sweet, respectful intimacy.

One thing strikes a visitor to any part of Mexico — but especially in Guadalajara, where you expect something different. This is the complete indifference to facts. Nobody knows whether the city has twenty thousand or two hundred thousand people; as a matter of fact, it has about one hundred and eighty thousand. No one knows whether the Cathedral is twenty or two thousand years old. And nobody cares. It is not an atmosphere wherein you take stock. The exact facts of life just do not matter. You take what the day brings.

It was given to us to visit many homes — homes of the old families with the barred windows on the sidewalk and the cool, lovely patios inside: homes of young American business men with mission furniture and Hollywood trappings; homes of the intellectuals built in the new style without patios and with front lawns; and at least one home of almost illimitable wealth. Forsaking the charming old architecture of the Spanish era, some of the newly rich of the revolutionary period have built a new addition to the city — the Colonia. Many of these fortunes have come with the suddenness of a desert thunder-shower. The new architecture in many cases is unspeakably awful. How any architect could look at those serene old churches and those lovely mansions in the old quarter and commit some of these horrors passes all understanding. The worst of them look like the offspring of a marriage between a Hollywood movie bungalow and the cover of a Christmas candy-box. Some of them have front lawns. I have an unreasoning prejudice against front lawns. Why should they have followed me to Guadalajara?

Just as in Sinaloa it had been permitted to me to come closely in contact with the life of the old haciendas, so in Guadalajara it came my way to be guest at a dinner attended by the aristocracy and beauty of Jalisco. The señora had been educated in a private school in Los Angeles. I had known her there. Her story is the story of modern Mexico. Young and beautiful, she has never known the meaning of money. It has been poured into her lap. The daughter of a very old Spanish family, dating back for centuries of Mexican life, her people have lived from the land. In Sinaloa they own an enormous plantation where her little-girl years were spent. In Sonora they have mines, and many of her memories are of the wild Yaquis who adored her distinguished father. In Michoacan, her brother has a great hacienda where five thousand

peons plant and reap his wheat. She has been educated
to the limit. Most of the modern languages ripple off
her tongue like music. She is married to a rarely handsome
and distinguished young man of one of the old families.
Nevertheless, I could sense that she was miserable. She
goes to her house in Mexico City; then to Europe; then to
Hollywood; then to the hacienda — looking for something
that she never can find.

'You are a caged tiger,' I said critically.

'Yes,' she agreed. 'Exactly. We entertain and entertain and entertain. When we do not entertain, my husband goes to bed at nine. Following the Spanish etiquette,
I then go to my room and for hours I walk up and down
the floor like your caged tiger. I feel that I will die if I
don't get out — and where is out?'

'What you need,' I said, 'is a job.'

She leaned eagerly over the table. 'Oh, for the love of
God, give me a job; it would save me!'

'What kind of a job?'

'Any kind of a job; anything to do. I must do something
or die. I am young and strong. I am not a fool. I have no
children. I have been educated. Where do I go from
here?'

'How would you like to write?'

'I would love it.'

'It could be arranged.'

'Then I am practically writing right now.'

The words of a Mexican professor with whom I had
foregathered in Mazatlan came back to me. 'The dawn
of a new day for Mexico will come,' he said, 'when the
peon woman stops grinding tortillas and begins buying
baker's bread. In other words, when the brains and the

strength of the Mexican women are released for something worth while.'

About twenty years ago, Mexico suddenly leaped out of the Middle Ages into the twentieth century. The wonder is, not that she has had so many revolutions, but that she has had so few. And that these revolutions have had so little destructive effect upon the slow, steady progress of the character of the people. The effect has been most marked upon the educated women of the better class. In search of clothes and excitement, they make little forays out of Mexico into other countries that have become essentially matriarchal; then they go home to a man's world. And never forget that Spanish Mexico had its roots in a remembered Moorish culture and civilization. The well-bred woman of Mexico two generations back lived the life of the châtelaine of a medieval castle. Her life was bound up in her family and a small circle of friends. Now she finds herself cut adrift from that and halfway into a new world where family life has ceased functioning and where nobody has any friends — just bridge partners. To her a railroad ticket represents a bridge between long centuries. The peon woman has been the balance wheel. Not having the price of a railroad ticket, she has edged her way along very slowly.

There are thoughtful minds in Mexico who see in the character of the Mexican peon the hope that Mexico may progress without falling into the fatal errors of neighboring civilizations. They are anxious, among other things, that the Mexican farmer shall continue to regard farming as a manner of life rather than a food factory. Most of all that, as machinery inevitably comes into his life, it shall remain a tool. That the machine shall be his servant rather than his master. Most of all that money shall remain something to spend rather than a goal to be struggled for, fought for, and prayed for. But above all else these enlightened men of better minds are anxious that the uninsistent little Latin-Indian shall not lose his balanced appreciation of the realities of life.

My Indian friends tell me that the white man has ruined his own happiness because he has departed from the world. He has built himself a world in which his horizon is a skyscraper; he walks on man-made pavements; he has surrendered his song to a machine; has lost his sense of sight and smell, and — most disastrous of all — has lost contact with the electric earth currents. The man whom we call primitive regards himself as one note in a grand symphony. The trees, the dumb animals, the rocks, are more than his brothers; they are his other self.

The peon stands between these theories of life. His future course is one of perilous uncertainty. I think he has less in life and more in life than any other man with whom I have come in contact. There is such a thing as getting so much that you have nothing. From outward appearances it would seem that no class of people have ever had so much as the favored children of Hollywood, for instance. It looks as though Fate had brought to them on a silver platter, like French pastry, all the blessings that men fight for — youth, beauty, fame, wealth. Yet, take them as a class, if there is a more miserably unhappy collection on the face of the earth, I should not know in which direction to seek them. Miss Lillian Gish and I — comparing notes — agreed that we did not know one happy person among the favored children of fortune of Hollywood. I cite Hollywood because it seems to be the ultimate of everything that our Anglo-Saxon civilization erects as a goal. The little peon of Mexico hasn't had many Christmas morning oranges; but he has not had the shattering tragedy of sucking them dry and finding them sour.

The woman of the type of our hostess has found herself adrift between the two worlds. The din of the jazz orchestras of Hollywood has drowned out the plaintive strum of the guitar; but she dimly realizes that jazz is the cadence of a Hottentot prayer — without any heathen god to pray to.

Dinner she said would be at 8.30. With railroad punctuality, I punched the electric bell at 8.29. No answer. I punched and punched until my thumb gave symptoms of collapse. I sat down on the steps for reflection; then rose to take another punch. At last a surprised butler in evening clothes opened the door and I managed to convince him that I was me. 'The señora,' he said vaguely, 'asks you to sit in the library. She has not yet dressed.' Time means nothing in Mexico. Dinner is when you get there, and you get there when you get there. Being a cook in Mexico must have complications. The interval permitted me to study one of the most beautiful houses I have ever seen. French Empire yet Mexican — a beautiful drawing-room opening into a flower-perfumed patio. Beyond the patio, the patio of the servants, still more like retainers than servants. They spoke to the señora with an easy affection under their formal respectful courtesy.

The guests were of the old aristocracy of Mexico. One was a handsome young matron from an old family at Guaymas. She looked like a Moorish princess. Everyone seemed to have been educated in Europe. They spoke

Spanish, French, or English as the topic came up. The dinner-table might have been set for a feast of Lucullus. The plate was of gold; likewise the goblets. All that was needed to complete the picture was to have led in a couple of captive emperors with strings through their noses.

The conversation was gay, cultured, and witty — but sometimes profound. No one else has come into my experience with charm equal to a cultured Mexican. Under his sophistication is a touch of occult mystery — always a little whisper of things unseen, an echo of ancient Aztec and Mayan rites.

The hostess told of the aged Maria, the bread peddler. She was a Yaqui. The señora encountered her first in a public market and she came thereafter to the house to sell Yaqui bread — which attracted a whim of the moment.

One day Maria was firmly insistent that bread must be bought even though the whim had passed. 'I have,' she said, 'to earn money for my children.'

'How many children have you, then?'

'Forty-two.'

'What, not really forty-two! No; you couldn't have; it is impossible!'

'The number,' said Maria firmly, 'is forty-two.'

'But where did you get them? Certainly you didn't ...'

'Battlefields,' she said briefly.

She explained that in the terrific Yaqui battles many children were left orphans. She went around and collected the left-overs.

'You have had to feed forty-two children all this while?'

'Sometimes not so many — sometimes twenty-five, thirty.'

'How is that?'

'When I find that I have more than I can feed, I kill a few,' said Maria. 'How much bread shall I give you, señora?'

'Maria,' gasped the señora, 'not really? You don't mean to tell me that you actually kill the children you cannot feed!'

'Certainly I kill them,' said Maria. 'What would you think of me, señora, if I allowed the poor little things to starve?'

One day there was a murder mystery in Guadalajara. They were discussing it with the usual excitement when Maria came in with the bread. She listened in, so to speak, until they got ready to pay attention to her bread.

'Oh,' she said, her eyes lighting up with sudden interest, 'you mean that man down there in the cornfield? I killed him.'

'Maria, what on earth are you talking about?'

'Were you not discussing a man found dead in the cornfield? He had revealed the hiding-place of one of our priests down in the Yaqui country. I saw him when I came here, so naturally I killed him. What would you?'

'Oh, yes — naturally,' murmured the señora.

One day Maria happened to arrive at the end of a tiresome tea-party. As the guests departed, one of the señora's young house guests exclaimed in the direction of the departing group of ladies, 'Oh, how I would like to kill that woman!'

The next time Maria arrived, another tea-party was assembling. Her quick Indian eyes took in the situation. She put down her bread-basket in a corner; pulled a long

knife from her stocking, and took up her station near the
front door.

'For God's sake, Maria!' screamed the señora. 'What
are you doing?'

'Show me which is the one you don't like,' said Maria
amiably. 'I will kill her as she comes in.'

Maria said that her father had been killed on a Yaqui
battlefield, but that she had his skull in her home as a
loving souvenir.

'His head? Good gracious! Where did you get his head?'

'I cut it off,' said Maria simply. 'After the battle, I
went out on the field and searched until I found him and
cut off his head. I loved my father very much and
wanted something to keep by me. So I cut off his head.'

'That was hard,' said the señora sympathetically.
'It must have been very hard for you.'

'Yes, it was a little hard,' conceded Maria. 'Especially
that big bone at the back of the neck. That was very
hard — very tough.'

It was a great relief to all concerned when Maria took
her brood back to the Yaqui country. There was too much
Roman matron in Maria.

The talk at dinner turned to the philosophy of experience as it applied to a lovely young woman who had
suffered from an unfortunate marriage, but was headed
for an encore. 'Having burned one's finger in the candle-
flame, one does not put one's finger back into the flame,'
said the hostess lightly. The young man at her right
leaned over and held his finger in the flame of one of the
table candles — a tall cathedral candle, shrugged his
shoulders, and put it back again into the flame — humor-
ously disproving her statement. I have known several

Indians who could do that with fire; never before a white man. In some way they surround the flesh with a protection of thought...

Later in the evening, in the drawing-room, one of the older men came across the room to me. 'When are you to start your book?' he asked.

'Book? I am not going to write a book,' I said. 'I don't write books. I write a column in a newspaper. When gentlemen get angry at their wives, they prop up my column against the sugar-bowl and pretend to be reading it. I supply the 'studied silence' that you read about in divorce courts.'

'Nevertheless,' he said gravely, 'you are going to write a book — many books. It will be the happiest period of your life.'

'How do you know all this? You have known me only about an hour.'

He hesitated. 'It is difficult for me to explain,' he said slowly. 'Does it mean anything to you when I say that you have come to the seventh period of your life?'

'Not a darn thing.'

'Then be content,' he said, smiling. 'And take my word for it that you are about to write a book.'

CHAPTER XIX

NOTES FROM MY GUADALAJARA DIARY

WHEN I came down from my room this morning, an amazing sight met my astonished eyes. One of the engineers had been dressing up Nicolas Pinta — El Norteño. Not that we would willingly have changed one breath or replaced one missing front tooth from the personality of Nicolas, but we could see that he felt embarrassed in his ragged hickory shirt and his guarachas, now that he was el secretario to the Gringo caballeros. Nicolas had, after heavy meditation, announced that he was the secretary of the expedition.

In his new clothes, his elegance was almost overwhelming. His charming old straw sombrero had been replaced by a collegiate lid whose ribbon was of such uproarious hue that you could feel it in the dark. His shirt and tie were a rebel yell, and his tan shoes the most fanciful and the tightest ever seen south of the Rio Grande. It was the first time his feet had ever known shoes, and he was dying by inches. He walked like a cat on a hot plate. His face under his jauntily cocked hat was both alarmed and agonized. But when I suggested that he take off the instruments of torture and put on his comfortable guaraches, he drew back indignantly. If he had to die, he was determined to die stylishly. I observed that for the rest of the day El Norteño remained in one of the automobiles. He said he had to stay there to guard it, but it was noticeable that he did not lift his feet where they could be seen. I had a suspicion that he was giving them a little surcease from sorrow.

One of the quaint sights of Guadalajara is the public letter-writer. They are to be found elsewhere in Mexico, but nowhere else in such profusion. Guadalajara must have a lot of letters to write. The scribes sit around long tables on a side street off the plaza and thump out the missives for the cash customers on aged typewriters. In the stories I have read about the public letter-writers of the Orient, they are always represented as inditing sweet messages of love. But the customers who sit at the elbows of these Guadalajara letter-writers appear to be sending directions for distant funerals and the letter-writers always seem to have been incredibly bored in early youth and to have been accumulating boredom ever since.

This afternoon we went to a bull-fight in the Plaza de los Toros. Over the rim of the amphitheater, towers of an old convent standing against the skyline. I had expected to see the wealth and fashion of Guadalajara in the seats on the shady side, but the expensive seats were half-empty and there were no belles. Bull-fighting seems to have ceased to be fashionable. Even the bulls did not appear to have much enthusiasm for the drama. One bull jumped over the barrier four times — looking for the way home. He was as lithe as a greyhound.

The matadors were second-rate artists. One of them wore a surgical plaster on his check where a bull had gored him the week before in Mexico City. He looked white and shaken. He haggled the bulls with his sword, never making a clean kill. Once he jabbed the espada into the animal's shoulder blade. The bull shook it off, hurling the sword into the grandstand.

There was, however, one real thrill. A toreador, coaxing away the bull from a fallen picador, missed his footing and fell flat. When he scrambled to his feet, it was too late to retreat behind the barrier. He backed off to the wall of the bull-ring — the worst place he could go — and stood with his arm raised before his face, instinctively trying to ward off the bull which was charging. His face wore an expression of dread and horror. There was a crash as the wall hit the bull's horns. To our surprise the toreador stood there unhurt. The bull happened to have extraordinarily long horns. They hit the wall on either side of the bull-fighter, leaving him unscathed inside a little pen of horns.

What impressed me about the bull-fight was the world-weary lack of zest. The crowds jeered weakly when the matador missed the kill. Instead of cringing from their jeers, his face wore the bitter expression of sneering resignation of a floor-walker in a department store being rebuked by the manager to satisfy the vanity of the offended Mrs. Moneybags.

The tamest part of the show were the picadors. They rode in on bored old horses who were gored to death on the horns of bulls who had to be aggravated to the goring. The horses struggled to their feet again with their bowels hanging out, but with a patient expression. It struck me as very pathetic to see how obediently they answered the slightest touch of the bit after this act of treachery on the part of their riders.

There was nothing heroic about the fall of the pica-dors. They were so padded with clothes and leather shields that a freight train could have run over them without hurting them much. When their horses fell, they lay helplessly in a wad of clothes until the other bull-fighters helped them up. They suggested nothing so much as a drunken old gentleman being hauled home by his scornful wife. The most interesting chap in the whole fight was a picador who violated all the traditions by refusing to allow his horse to be gored by the bull. Each time the nag was summoned to the slaughter, the picador planted his long pike in the bull's bloody shoulder and held him there. If the bull charged, he only forced the horse to back off. The bull — thus stopped in his tracks — glared around at the circle of toreadors in puzzled embarrassment as though to say: 'Well, what do you suppose one does in a case like this?'

There were, however, points of unexpected interest in the fight. I was interested to see how the matador stepped out alone and studied the bull when he first came out from the dark pen. No fooling. Bull-fighting is playing tag with death. The ability to size up the character of that bull may be the difference between life and death for the matador.

Another thing that impressed me was the fact that the matador advances to the kill only after the bull has come to the point where he says: 'Well, say, what's this all about, anyhow? I am tired of hooking a lot of red flags that have nothing behind them.'

The final point of drama to me was the puzzled look that came into the eyes of the bull as, with the sword up to the hilt in his vitals, he stood with his forefeet planted and blood gushing from his mouth, unable to understand the strange weakness that was taking his life away.

In the afternoon we went to pay a call of ceremony and state to the Governor of Jalisco, of which state Guadalajara is the capital. The engineers wanted to secure his coöperation in a great highway plan.

The Governor's office is in a great palace. It is one of the most beautiful and most interesting buildings in Mexico. It was built in 1643. Here Miguel Hidalgo y Castilla sketched and wrote the declaration of independence from Imperial Spain. Here in March, 1858, Benito Juarez narrowly escaped assassination at the hands of a lunatic. The palace has played a great part in the long drama of Mexico.

Like many other Mexicans of the new régime, the Governor who ruled Jalisco at the time of our visit was a self-made man. He had been a vaquero, and even then walked with the odd, rocking, uncertain gait of one who has spent his time in the saddle and whose walking has been done on high-heeled vaquero boots.

The Governor received us in a magnificent palatial room from the walls of which the dead heroes of Mexico looked down upon us. We sat in a row of chairs at one side of the room. The Governor and his staff sat in a row of chairs on the other side. A servant brought in champagne, and we asked after the health of the Governor. Another servant brought in cognac, and he asked after our health. He said the State of Jalisco was honored by our presence. We said we were honored by his words. Then we retired, and he turned the proposition down cold and flat.

CHAPTER XX
THE TOWN OF THE POTTERS

CAN you imagine what would happen if our Federal Farm Relief Board went to the crop sufferers in some Iowa or Arkansas town with this proposition: 'We have a way out of your difficulties. Now that you are not making a living out of your farms, why not let the farms go and put in your time on one of the creative fine arts?' Yet there are two towns near Guadalajara in which the inhabitants are doing just that. The towns are San Pedro Tlaquepaque and Tonala. In these two towns the one form of industry is creative art — pottery. Literally everyone is a born artist.

The Mexicans are an amazing people in this regard. They drink in art with their mother's milk. If you will send away your wife who thinks she knows on a vacation and leave your landscaping to the Mexican who comes to hoe your garden, the result will be good for your soul. In California I had a peculiarly perplexing problem of a terraced lot that dipped into a little barranca where a house was to be built. In a moment of high inspiration, I grabbed the first Mexican day laborer who came to hand and gave him carte blanche. He was an old fellow named Juan. The result was something very charming and interesting. My reputation for culture and good taste and artistic vision has glowed in the hearts of my friends ever since. In the Mexican National Museum there is a tiny napkin admired by thousands as a work of delicate and lovely artistry. It was made by an old peon woman to keep the flies off the tortillas she was peddling.

When the Spanish Conquistadores came first into the present State of Jalisco, they found the people of Tonala making pottery of rare beauty. The great-great-great-great-grandsons and daughters are still making pottery of rare beauty. I was just about to say they were making it from the same designs, but they have no designs. They make up the designs as they go along, as a true artist should. That's the wonderful thing about their work. They sit in the doorways of their adobes with an earthen jar in their hands and a little brush of dog's hair. They make the designs as they go. They do not even pencil them out, yet so accurate is their instinct that, as they turn the jars round and round following the design, the figures all fit — always meet on the far side with mathematical accuracy.

Sometimes the whole family works at the job. You see them sitting in circles in the adobe doorways or in the little patios, quiet and contented. That little town of the potters snuggled into my heart. In traffic jams with a thousand automobiles spitting out poison carbon monoxide, when the desk telephone rings and the town clatters and roars around me until I am one lap from the insane asylum, I think of the little peasants of Tonala, sitting in the dirt and the dust and fleas, in their white cotton clothes and their bare feet, a beautiful work of art taking shape in their hands and a gentle serenity in their faces. We are a mad people, straining and pushing and throat-cutting and tricking and double-crossing — and what have we that the little gentle people of art in Tonala have not?

I gained philosophy from an old man in Tonala.

IN TONALA, THE TOWN OF THE POTTERS

'Why, señor, do you hurry, hurry, hurry?'

'Well — um — er — I hope to achieve something in life.'

'Achieve? What is that, señor?'

'Well, don't you see — maybe if I hurry, I could get famous or something.'

'What is famous?'

'Why, you know — where everybody talks about you.'

'Everybody would talk about you if you had three legs or six fingers.'

Feeling compelled me to re-form my defenses. I said: 'I hurry that I may not starve in my old age.'

'Don't your children and your friends like you?'

'I don't know; perhaps they like me well enough.'

'Would they, then, let you starve?'

'Well, you see it's like this,' I said desperately. 'They will have their own burdens when I get old. As a matter of pride I do not wish to live on their bounty. Therefore, I hurry, hurry, hurry.'

'You have strange ideas, señor,' he observed. 'You would rather hurry, hurry, hurry, and make yourself miserable for sixty-five or seventy years rather than endure the small and brief discomfort of starving, which — at the most — would be a matter of ten or twelve days.'

I don't suppose that Tonala is an Elysium, but you can't walk those little narrow, dirty streets, between the rows of peaceful adobes, and watch the pottery painters with their cotton drawers and their dog's-hair brushes without thinking of Kipling's lines:

And no one shall work for money, and no one shall work for fame,
But each for the joy of working, and each in his separate star
Shall draw the Thing as he sees it for the God of Things as They are.

secret. She found the bewitched figure of her son. Working with furious haste — and being no mean potter herself — she made a figure exactly like Pablo's cursed work, except that the middle was not ossified. Then she made another secret visit; substituted her figure of Pedro for the taboo. Safely outside, she smashed the witch figure on a stone. Pedro slept peacefully that night. In the morning he had taken a marked turn for the better. In a few days he was well, his stomach and bowels having returned to the job.

Pablo, expecting to find him dead, met Pedro blithely walking along the street. Embracing his enemy, the wicked Pablo begged to be forgiven. 'I have tried to kill one whom the gods have taken under their personal protection,' he said. To Pablo's immeasurable relief, Pedro forgave him on the spot. Ever since then they have been the best of friends.

I shall never forget the blind street minstrel of Tonala. He was a sad old man with a guitar. He was led around the streets by a ragged little boy who sat on the ground and threw pebbles at marks while the old man sang. We asked him to sing this and that for us, and it struck me afterward that the songs we asked for were not only grotesquely inappropriate, but a little cruel in the circumstances. He sang them all in the flat, lusterless voice of the blind. Most of them were gay little songs of love and romance... *Cielito Lindo* and *Negra Consentida* and *Estrellita*. I wondered, as he sang, if the songs called to his blind eyes the visions that they called to mine — of señoritas with flashing black eyes seen under lace mantillas, of little red heels on satin shoes that clicked through the measures of the jarabe and the jota. And how strange it must have seemed to him, hearing voices in a strange, unknown tongue calling for these songs, and having coins larger than he had ever felt dropping from the mystery of the eternal night of his sightlessness into his hands!

Near Tonala is the old town of San Pedro Tlaquepaque. It is also a pottery town, but rather touristy. Before the first of the twenty-year series of revolutions deposed Porfirio Diaz, San Pedro was a fashionable suburb of Guadalajara. Remnants of the glory remain in the form of quintas — suburban villas — of great elegance and luxury. One especially remains in my memory.

You enter the heavy studded front door into a sort of loggia which was part foyer, part living-room for the family. It opened directly into an enormous patio, a great courtyard in which a battalion of troops could be maneuvered. In some of the large quintas, a huerta — a family orchard — stands behind the wall of the patio. In this case, the huerta was in a side patio down upon which you could look from some of the bedrooms.

Around the courtyard were the rooms of the establishment. On one side were the quarters of the servants, who must have been a young army. On another side, the kitchens, laundries, and storehouses. On a fourth side were the apartments of the more intimate retainers of the family. The house itself was in two stories, the master bedrooms being on the upper floor. The courtyard had an enormous gate which could be thrown open to admit wagons and teams, then closed for defense. A high wall surrounded the courtyard.

In looking these places over, I was struck by the difference between them and the old California houses I had seen. The California ranch-houses were all low one-story adobes built around patios. They suggest peace and intimacy — simple homes in a country where everyone was literally a cousin of everyone else — and where there was nothing to fear. All Mexican houses, on the other hand, suggest danger and tragedy — heavy studded doors, fortress gates, bullet-torn towers, death, tears, blood, and tragedy.

Guadalajara has other alluring suburban places. One of these is Zapopan. There is an old church and monastery that have more flavor than is to be found anywhere else I know of in Mexico. In August, it has one of the most interesting cermonies to be found in the country. In front of the monastery, which was built in the seventeenth century, is a great courtyard. During this celebration in August, the Indians go into camp there. A lodging for the night is a simple process for the Indian tourists. They wrap up in a serape and squat up against the wall — with the missus and the kids. On the great day, the faithful come from their homes in Guadalajara and they come on their knees — a twenty-minute journey on a street car. All day long — and sometimes all day and all night — they come edging along on their knees, praying and telling their beads as they come. It is custom and etiquette to spread a blanket or a serape — in the fashion of Sir Walter Raleigh — for their poor knees to rest on a moment if you pass them in the road.

The climax of the festival is a native pageant — a representation of the story of the conquest of Jalisco by the Spanish, presumably to call the attention of the Saints of the Sky to the dirty deal the Indians had at the hands of the Conquistadores. The Indians take the parts both of the Indians who suffered and of the Spanish knights at whose hands they suffered. A little Jalisco Indian, dressed up as a Spanish knight and talking in the way he thinks the knights must have talked, is something not to be forgotten.

CHAPTER XXI

A MEXICAN EASTER

EASTER WEEK came while we were in Guadalajara. The festival was of unusual significance that year. For two or three years the priests had been in exile. Some of them had been hunted down and killed. Others had been driven out. During this period the faithful had worshiped by themselves in the dim old churches. I had seen them during this period. It was poignant drama. I had seen old women crawling in on their knees over rough country roads to the churches, prostrating themselves to the last rags of humility, that God might be moved by their sorrow and send them back their priests. In the cathedral at Guadalajara I had seen young girls kneeling before the altars with crowns of thorns on their heads. I had seen peons standing for hours in the silent churches with arms outstretched — expressions of rapt devotion in their dark eyes, standing in the position of Christ on the Cross, imploring God to relent and send back their priests.

And now it was Easter and the priests had come back.

Judas was hanged on every street-corner in revenge for his mortal sin. The Judas is as much a part of a Mexican Easter as the painted Easter egg is of our Easter. The Judas is usually a doll of grotesque ugliness. These dolls range all the way from tiny pocket-sized souvenirs to enormous dangling effigies that are strung across the streets on ropes like election banners. Judas is shot and kicked and burned and jeered. It suggests nothing so much as an American crowd yelling at the umpire at a baseball game.

With the beginning of Holy Week, the church bells of the city were stilled. The faithful were called to worship by the clatter of wooden wheels slapping on wood clappers. Curtains had been dropped over the holy images in the churches. By Wednesday it had become like a city of the dead. A hush seemed to fall over the streets. The taxicabs honking at the corners sounded like voices in a tomb. Even the sedate old horses dragging the quaint little open park carriages seemed to go slower — if that were possible.

Miercoles de Ceniza — Ash Wednesday... the Holy Drama was rising to an intense climax.

Jueves Santo — Holy Thursday — the night of the 'Visitar los Monumentos,' when each penitent must visit seven different churches and make the Stations of the Cross — the time before Easter when Holy Communion may be taken.

Word had come to me that the Archbishop of Jalisco, one of the great lords of the Mexican Catholic Church, would receive me at his home — Francisco Orosco Jimenez. He was a lovely, gentle old man with a handsome, patrician face — a regal bearing, but a manner of winning simplicity. We were ushered into his presence in a splendid old drawing-room with deep recessed windows and cool, deep shadows. He was a very old man and his face was white with fatigue. We knew he had not eaten that day, so we shook his hands while our guide, like a good Catholic, knelt to kiss the seal ring of the Archbishopric. Then we prepared to withdraw. 'No, no,' he said in the quaint precise English of one who had learned it from a book and a library, 'you must not go. I do not want you to go.' Several times we rose to take our leave, but each time his thin, ascetic, beautiful hands pushed us back into our chairs. 'Do you want me to be cross with you?' he asked. 'Then sit down. I do not want you to go.'

It was the hour of his quiet triumph. He told us that the year before he had celebrated Easter Mass in the darkened room of a lonely adobe house hidden in the mountains, conducting the service almost in whispers, with one priest to assist. 'As you well know,' he said to the Mexican gentleman who had conducted us into his presence. We also smiled, for we knew that it was this faithful friend who had carried news and food to the hiding-place during those days of peril. Daring death, not at the hands of the Government, but of bands of fanatics.

'And now,' said the Archbishop, smiling.

And now we knew that on Easter morning there was to be a magnificent High Pontifical Mass, with fifty priests assisting the Archbishop.

When we finally insisted on leaving, in order that he might rest before the ordeal of the afternoon, the Archbishop got up with us and showed us over the old house. It was an interesting type of a city house of the aristocracy of an earlier day. It belonged to a family named Moreno. It had been tendered to him as a home until a new palace could be arranged. It was a charming old place of strange, unexpected passageways, lovely old worn stone stairways that twisted and turned in and out of little balconies. The Archbishop's study was a bare little cell at the top of the house, bare save for a rawhide bed, a simple table and a Holy Crucifix.

That afternoon, by the Archbishop's special invitation,

we attended one of the most interesting of all ceremonies
of Easter week — the Washing of the Feet. The cathedral was crowded to the doors. But a Mexican crowd
lacks the football instincts of an American crowd. Everyone stood patiently where he found himself. Except ourselves. Magic hands seemed to open a way for us through
the press until we found ourselves at last inside the chancel
rail in the sanctuary.

The ceremony was long and intricate and beautiful.
It ended with the Archbishop washing the feet of twelve
old men who sat in a row in front of the altar. In theory
they had been picked up on the street. One was an old
peon in white cotton pants and guarachas. Another was
a fat old man with an imitation gold watch-chain across
his shabby vest. One was a dignified old gentleman with
a cane; his face bore the marks of better days. One was
plainly of Indian blood. They were embarrassed and very
miserable, but I was interested to see how quietly they
could sit and still be obviously ill at ease. Their bodies
were absolutely motionless during the whole ceremony,
and they did not fiddle with their hands. Their faces were
inscrutable and without expression. Yet I felt that they
were wretchedly unhappy at having an Archbishop wash
their feet.

Just before the climax of the ceremony, the magnificence
of the Archbishop's robes had been changed to a simple
vestment of white, signifying purity and humility. A
little processional started at one end of the line of twelve
who sat, each with one foot bare — those pathetic old
bare feet with their ludicrous big toes. Several priests
followed the Archbishop down the line of feet. One carried a large silver pitcher; another, a basin. The basin

was put on the floor under each foot, and the priest with
the pitcher poured out a tiny stream of water over the
bare foot. A third priest handed the Archbishop a cloth,
a beautiful linen towel edged with Mexican drawn-work.
With this he wiped the water from the uplifted foot and
bent to press his lips upon the flesh. I have never seen
anybody look more utterly miserable than the peasant
whose foot was being kissed.

That afternoon all of Guadalajara's fifty odd churches
were thronged with penitents waiting to confess their
sins in preparation for Easter. There were many touches
of poignant and pathetic drama. In the old sixteenth-
century church of San Francisco sat an old, old man waiting for the priest. His bullet-shaped head was white; his
face, worn and tired. Finally, a door opened at the rear
of the church and a priest in brown robes came out. He,
too, was very, very old. His withered skin was like parch-
ment. He did not go to one of the confessionals. He took
his seat on a rough wooden bench, worn with age. He
beckoned to the old penitent, who crossed the dim church
and knelt by the bench. Tears were running down his
deep-furrowed cheeks. He sank to his knees, and his tears
ran down into the lap of the priest's coarse brown Fran-
ciscan robe. For a while the priest laid one delicate,
ascetic hand on the old man's head and allowed him to
cry. Then he bent his head to listen to the confession.
Their two old whitened heads were together. The penitent
held his lips close to the priest's head and whispered so for
a long time. Now and then the priest would nod his
head as though in understanding. At last, the story
finished, the old man who was confessing knelt with bent
head waiting for his answer. The priest sat in silence for

a moment. Then he spoke quietly; made the sign of the Cross; rose and walked back to the room from which he had come and shut the door. The old man remained kneeling for a while at the bench. Then he rose stiffly and wearily to his feet and walked back to the rear of the church, where he knelt again on the old, old tiles that had so often been wet with tears. The last I saw of him, he was telling the beads of his rosary and the tears were wet on his cheeks and upon his mumbling lips.

That night the Visitar los Monumentos. Each faithful Catholic visited seven different churches, saying the prayers of the Way of the Cross in each church. It was a ceremony touching and interesting. Often whole families made the round together. One such group we met in church after church that night. The group consisted of a bent old grandmother, her son and daughter-in-law and their four children. One was a girl of about eighteen. In Spanish she read aloud the ritual of their prayers and litanies — the story of the Christ and His divine sacrifice. They knelt in front of each station; prayed while she read aloud from the book. Then on to the next sacred image. And so on through seven great dim churches with their veiled altars, the faint, musty smell of old buildings cut by the acrid odor of incense.

The cathedral, with its great Byzantine towers which dominate the city, its paintings by the old masters; San Francisco, with its ancient Baroque façade and its pigeons; El Carmen, with its allegoricals done by native Indians; Jesus Maria, with its famous Santisima Virgen del Rayo; the Santuario de Nuestra Señora de Guadalupe... My favorite of all is one of the smallest churches, the little old Church of Our Lady of Aranzazu, with its golden

altar and its quaint figure of the Christ with false hair.
Gold used in decoration is pretty awful, but gold in mass
like this altar is beautiful and impressive. Santa Monica,
with its crude statues, one of which was used in olden times
by bandits as a hiding-place for their loot — churches and
churches and churches...

CHAPTER XXII

THE LAKE COUNTRY

ONE always thinks of Mexico as a country of sagebrush, deserts, skinny cow-ponies, and horned toads. On Easter morning we started through a Mexico of great pine forests, crystal lakes, wheatfields, and fine horses.

Some day, this part of Mexico will become one of the great tourist resorts of the world. It has everything — wild, picturesque beauty, history, tradition, interest, romance — all, thus far, unspoiled by tourist hotels, dude ranches, and radio announcers.

Just out from Guadalajara, climbing to the high plateaus, we rode through an interesting sociological experiment. It is a great tract of land subdivided into model farms. Model farmhouses — more like Hollywood cottages than old-time Mexican ranch-houses — have been built as part of the movement to put the peon on his own land.

At which point, I now proceed to run for my life. There are two subjects to be avoided in Mexico as one avoids scorpions and rattlesnake poison. These are the agrarian question and the labor question. Both are loaded with dynamite. Perhaps one may take a desperate chance and say simply this: that after the revolution which deposed Porfirio Diaz, the movement was started to cut up the big haciendas and distribute the land among the peasants. The hacendados contend that what has been the property of their families through many generations has been wrested from them without right; that the peasants do not know how to farm or manage the land after they get it, and that they end in cultivating enough corn for the family tortillas and the rest lies idle. The contention of the agrarian is that the land titles of the hacendados have no real basis in justice, law, or equity, and that the peon cannot be blamed for his lack of ability as a farm executive. He will progress as Mexico progresses.

The labor question is one still more bitter. The employers claim that the labor laws are harsh and oppressive. The laborers claim that only by such regulation have they been set free from slavery. You can roll your own conclusion; that cloud of dust flying down the road is me.

The road from Guadalajara leads to Lake Chapala, one of the most charming and beautiful places on the American continent. The playground of the city of Guadalajara, Chapala, is the scene of D. H. Lawrence's novel, 'The Plumed Serpent.' The English novelist was one of the first to examine the soul of the Mexican peon. He recorded shrewd and brilliant conclusions about them in his novel: 'Women were coming up between the trees on the patch from the lake with jars of water on their shoulders; children were playing around the doors, squatting with their naked little posteriors in deep dust; and here and there a goat was tethered. Men in soiled clothes were lounging, with folded arms and one leg crossed in front of the other, against a corner of the house or crouching under the walls. Not by any means dolce far niente. They seemed to be waiting — eternally waiting for something.'

Again he makes one of his characters say: 'Mexico is like an old, old egg that the Bird of Time laid long ago: and she has been sitting on it for centuries till it looks foul in the nest of the world. But still it is a good egg.

It is not addled. Only the spark of fire has never gone into
the middle of it to start it.'

He speaks of the Mexican's strange indifference to
death. 'They are strong to carry heavy loads, but they
die easily. They eat all the wrong things and they don't
mind dying. They have many children, and they like
their children very much, but when the child dies, the
parents say, "Ah, he will be an angelito." So they cheer
up and feel as if they had been given a present.'

He speaks of a dance where the dancers were artisans,
mechanics, or railroad porters. No peons danced. 'Before very long the organdie butterflies and the flannel-
trouser fifis gave in, succumbed, crushed once more beneath the stone-heavy passivity. Down on it all, like a
weight of obsidian, comes the passive negation of the
Indian. He understands soul which is not of the blood,
but spirit, which is superior and is the quality of our civilization, this in the mass he darkly and barbarically repudi-
ates. Not until he becomes an artisan or connected with
machinery does the modern spirit get him...

'And against the dark flow of the Indian, the white
man at last collapses; with his God and his energy he
collapses.'

Although many Mexicans laugh at the 'Winged Serpent,' it is true that in the deeper phases of Mexican life
one always has the sense of a people waiting for a terrific
and mysterious Past to overtake them.

One of the great artists of Mexico has a school, attended
by many young children of Indian ancestry. To one who
came to him with pleading dark eyes, he said: 'My little
dear one, in your heart are the whispered memories of
the most remarkable race of artists who ever lived on this

earth. I would not have the impertinence to try to tell you how to paint pictures. See, here is paint and here is a brush.' The work of this child has since been seen in the great art galleries of Europe. Even in the ironic caricatures of young Covarubias — a sophisticate of sophisticates — there are wild, untamed memories. I do not know whether people are born again in new bodies, but the spirits of the great Aztec, Toltec, and Mayan civilizations are slipping back again to finish the saga interrupted by blood and conquest.

The West Coast of Mexico, along which we had been traveling, has always been a military frontier, an affair of the outposts to which professional soldiers had been sent to lonely garrisons to fight back the natives while the engineers explored the hills for gold. The country to which we had now come had always been a more or less settled country — a country of memories and mystery, a country where the wind in the wheat seems to whisper in strange, forgotten tongues.

We passed quaint little villages with old weather-beaten churches — on this Easter morning thronged with peasants. In one old town was a strange, eight-sided monument, ornate with figures and sacred carvings erected to the memory of one of the Popes. La Barca is a quaint little old town on the banks of a sleepy river which forms the boundaries of the states of Jalisco and Michoacan. The rural committee had been waiting at La Barca for us for hours. They led us on a formal ride through a city park planted with camphor trees and brought us finally to a grove where a table had been set out under the trees. It was charming.

A splendid banquet of young goats' flesh and tortillas

and frijoles and goodness knows what was cooking in an oven made of stones. The cook was an old Southern mammy. She was a thin old darkey with snow-white hair and skinny, claw-like hands and the plaintive melancholy of her race. You would expect to find her in a bandana making beaten biscuits, but here she was making fiery hot dishes in a strange land. She had forgotten her own language and looked at us uncomprehendingly when we spoke to her in English. She, of all the people at the party, seemed to take no interest whatever in us. To her it was another job. Her story was easy to reconstruct — a handsome young soldier in a Mexican garrison on the border and a likely mulatto gal from the cotton-fields of Texas — then a lifetime of exile in a strange land. She cooked one of the best dinners I ate in Mexico.

As we ate, the village orchestra came to the side of the table and played. The musicians were not like the gay fat fellows we had seen in Northern Mexico. There were four players. The leader was a young violinist with a delicate, ascetic face and long black hair that poured down over his face until he shook it back. The cornetist was an old, old man, almost in rags. There was a younger man with an ancient 'cello. He had broken off the spike which supported it on the ground, so he had hung it around his neck with a rope. The fourth member of the orchestra was a young boy with a guitar. For our benefit they had learned American tunes and laboriously and painfully fiddled out that infernal ditty from Tin-Pan Alley, 'Show Me the Way to Go Home.' They sighed with relief when we sent word by El Norteño to ask them to play only Mexican music. They could play anything. One piece for which we asked they had never heard of, whereupon a member of the reception committee left the table and went over to hum it to them. The young leader nodded gravely and began to play it — with the other musicians 'following' as though that had been their orchestra *pièce de résistance* all the days of their lives.

While the luncheon was still going on, another orchestra, this one of Mexican gypsies, whirled in from another town. With a most patronizing air they took the center of the stage while the little ragged orchestra retired behind a big camphor tree and listened with patient, unresentful resignation.

I watched the face of the old Negro woman while this little drama was going on. She continued to plod back and forth from her barbecue oven in the ground to the banquet table without one human sign of interest. Only the deep melancholy of her race. It was an interesting vignette of primitive racial contrasts — of the peasants of two races which have suffered bitterly and endured while bound to the soil; who have been in virtual slavery and who have worn out the fetters that bound them. The Negro has emerged with a deep, melancholy resignation through which bursts an unquenchable gayety of heart: emerged with a religious emotion that expresses itself in wailing spirituals that plead for a Paradise with golden chariots and fancy harps. The Mexican has emerged also with a resignation that is an acceptance of the dictates of God; but he is a rebel against men. The emotion of the Mexican heart is expressed in songs of a witty and sardonic humor; in fine irony and withering ridicule. I couldn't imagine a Mexican singing a spiritual. He clings to the hope of celestial life that will be his reward for suffering, but he neither hopes for nor expects fanciful heavens with gold streets. His religion is an obedient homage to a divine ruler — to the celestial commander-in-chief. He stands in silence with outstretched arms in his church, torturing himself with penitential fatigue or whispers his prayers in dim old cathedrals to El Señor Jesus — Christ the Master. The songs of the Negro are the songs of his servitude in the cotton-fields. The songs of the Mexican are songs of a freed soil — like *Cuatro Milpas* — that tell of a soldier's return to his cornfield ruined by the Revolution. There is always a suggestion of death in almost everything a Mexican does. He always marches to war yelling Death to somebody or other. Yet to him death is relatively nothing.

The more you know about Indians, the better you can understand the Mexican peon, for the roots of his being are Indian. Yet there is an essential difference. There is the same element of masked sarcastic humor; the same touch of sardonic malice. But in the case of the Mexican, it is a mask of courtesy — a charming smile that goes to the lips and is not of the eyes. In the case of the Navajo, the Sioux, or the Apache, it is a mask of open scorn. The American Indian would never and could never have endured the bitter slavery and oppression of the Spanish Conquest. He would have died fighting. The final irony accomplished by the Mexican Indian is that he is breeding into extinction and oblivion the races that kept him in slavery. The one hope of survival of the proud war peoples of the plains is in merging quietly into the white races. The Mexican Indians are reasonably certain of holding the trenches until the day when Mexico is virtually an Indian nation. It will be a great day. It is good blood.

When modern highways are built, this route that we

traveled will be thronged with tourist cars. We had long days on wonderful panoramas, lakes and glorious mountains — a crystal fairy lake called Canecuaro hidden by willows. We were paddled out across its clear depths by an Indian in a boat that was a hollowed-out log. It was a place for naiads who live in deep waters... and again a valley where sulphur springs come bubbling out of the ground furiously hot... a vivid green lake on a high hill in the crater of an extinct volcano... dreary little villages that seemed to have no reason for being there... roads turned to sticky gruel in the heavy rains... bands of musicians waiting to welcome us to tiny, sad pueblos... fields of waving wheat... landscapes like Turner paintings seen from hilltops... stone houses... the gates of great haciendas... villages of sullen, sardonic Indians where not a Mexican face was to be seen... ox-carts... burros... peon horsemen mounted on superb steeds... sombreros... dark faces... sashes... spurs...

And at last Zamora. This is an interesting old city which in the rainy season is marooned from the rest of Mexico. It has two old churches which rear themselves over the town with an ancient splendor of bell-towers and weathered walls. There is the inevitable plaza and the inevitable band; and around the plaza an arcade of shops — scarlet serapes hanging against the adobe walls, guarachas stacked on the sidewalk, sombreros on the shelves, candies in little glass boxes, saddles and silver bridles...

We were escorted in state to a hotel, where the stairways to the second floor run up from a charming old patio. My bedroom fronted on a street that was a processional of Old Mexico — packed burros weaving their way through the traffic; grave-looking peons with serapes hanging over their shoulders and huge sombreros tilted down over their eyes; women in open doorways; lovely young girls making their demure way down the sidewalk, watching the Gringo cars out of the corners of dark eyes with shy curiosity. Farther north in Sonora the señoritas are not so different from our own flappers; but in these mountain valleys they are still the señoritas of the Spanish Conquest.

The sweet old criada raps at the door of my room, asking me if she can help me in any way. I am only half-dressed, but the Mexicans have no mawkish modesty. She insists on helping me drag off my heavy field boots. She has only one English word — 'Flit.' I take a look at the bed, which is a little fortress guarded by mosquito-netting. 'Sí; gracias, señora. Flit.' She gallops off after the Flit. She not only sprinkles the whole room and all the crannies, but crawls under the bed on her hands and knees in relentless pursuit of the enemy. Her gratitude has a note of surprise when I give her a half-peso — cincuenta centavos. The Mexican peasants are sweet. When we leave the hotel next morning, she is there to say Goodbye, but waits bashfully until I say, 'Vaya con dios, señora,' before she has the temerity to say that lovely phrase. She has the shy timidity of a little girl, yet I know she would face death without a tremor — without an expression in her inscrutable, calm eyes.

All the grandees of the town were on hand for dinner, which was served at a long table under a portico at the edge of the patio. I sat next a young fellow who was general manager of the water company. I mentioned his excellent English, and he told me that he had lived in Los Angeles; had been educated at a Los Angeles business college. His people had been among the refugees driven from Mexico at the time of the overthrow of Porfirio Diaz.

'Providence works for good in his own way,' he said. 'There is nothing so important in the world, señor, as that there should be a complete understanding between Mexico and the United States. Europe is dying in her ashes — in her old hatreds. It is for our two countries to make a new world over here. Nature has given us everything but understanding. That is for us to work out. It is being worked out in two ways — by the Mexican boys who go to the United States as children and return here with a complete appreciation of your people. The other way is through the American travelers who are coming to Mexico to look and understand and go home to relate what they have seen. They are coming in increasing numbers every year and are going home — knowing what is in our hearts.'

He said he was doing what he could to bring modern business conditions into his work in this placid old town. But he wistfully confessed that he wished he were back in California. He was happy; yes, he thought he was happy; nevertheless, it was nice in Hollywood. 'I like the people of the United States,' he said. 'They have warm hearts and quick sympathies. They have biff and bang and pep, yet they are human and very kind.'

The contrasts of Old Mexico are a never-ending delight. That night we walked down the ancient streets and across the plaza at the hour of the paseo — when the señoritas walk in one direction, the gallant young caballeros in the opposite direction, passing and repassing, the old, old hour of the flirtations — a custom as old as the Moorish invasion of Spain. We went through the paseo, through old studded doorways to a patio that had been the middle of a long-forgotten inn — there to see two teams of college boys playing a furious game of basketball with the 'rah, 'rah, 'rahs, coaches on the sidelines and outbursts from the cheering fans — and fannettes.

CHAPTER XXIII

THEY CAME BEFORE THE AZTECS

THE next day we rode through a country peopled by strange and ancient gods. The Tarasco Indians can fairly defend themselves from any possible charge that they are tenderfeet in the country. They are old settlers. They were here in the lake country of Michoacan before the Aztecs came wandering down from the north — a half-savage hunter people.

The Aztecs came; endured a species of slavery; fought their way to freedom like the Children of Israel; built a mighty empire; were wiped out. But the Tarascos are still living in their little stone villages — scornful, contemptuous, and unmoved. Aztec, Spanish knight, Mexican, Gringo — they all look equally unimportant to the Tarasco.

Were I an artist trying to figure out a picture that would represent 'Contempt,' my model would be a little Tarasco Indian boy who hitch-hiked a ride on the back of one of our cars. We had been riding all morning through the Tarasco villages — eleven in all — little houses of stone crowded together on narrow, rocky roads; back of them a landscape of surpassing beauty; wind rippling through wheatfields backed by great mountains heavy with timber. The Tarasco women sat in the doorways and watched with malicious scorn. They looked like Apaches — billowing calico skirts ten yards wide. They watched as though we were bugs — and not a desirable variety of bug.

A boy about twelve hooked a ride on one of the cars, perching himself inside the extra tire. In the car immediately behind sat a colonel of the Mexican army — an aide of the Governor of Michoacan, a potentate. The colonel shouted a sharp order for the boy to get off the car. The little Indian gave him a glance of calm insolence; then looked away to a leisurely contemplation of the landscape. The colonel raved and roared, standing up in the car and shaking his impotent fists. To tell the truth, he looked as though he were about to disintegrate from spontaneous combustion. The little Indian glanced at him again with casual interest and curiosity; then retired into his own philosophic contemplations. At last, when the free ride had begun to lose its zest, he slid off and waited at the roadside for the colonel's car to come up. The colonel stopped the car and screamed a torrent of denunciation at the boy, who stood there, erect and proud and withering in his contempt. When the colonel had absolutely exhausted his vocabulary and his larynx, the boy threw the end of his serape back over his shoulder, turned coolly and contemptuously away — to walk back to his village. All of which is probably to be classified as one of the reasons why the Tarascos are an unconquered people.

In one of the oldest of these Tarasco towns, the inhabitants make a very interesting kind of glazed pottery. Long before the arrival of the invading Aztecs in Mexico, there was a race called the Toltecs of whom little is known — except that they were master craftsmen. Toward the end of their reign in the Valley of Mexico, they came wandering north into Michoacan. Here they encountered the Tarascans; taught them some of their arts — among them the art of making this glazed pottery.

I went up to a group of Indian women, watching us from the end of one of the dingy old streets. I showed them that I wanted to buy some glazed pottery. They turned away and scurried into the house — but did not come back with glazed pottery. Finally, I found a boy who was playing a lone game of tossing a basketball into a basket, with his serape over his shoulder. He was obviously bored, but finally, at my request, stopped a woman who was carrying a magnificent glazed bowl under her arm. He made known my wants. She did not even hesitate, but continued her walk. 'She doesn't care to sell you any pottery,' he said indifferently, as he went back to his basketball. On the whole I don't feel that I was exactly what you could call a social riot with the Tarasco Redskins.

Zacapu is hoary with romance and mystery as well as age. The town lies in the lee of a hill. On the hill stands a blockhouse like a fortress of the Middle Ages. The story of this hill runs back to a time before there was history. To stand under the hill of Zacapu is like standing in the shadows of Mount Olympus in Greece.

On these hills there once lived a long-forgotten tribe of hunter people. They were ruled by a king named Ticatamé who was half a god. Under his direction, the tribe moved restlessly on down the valleys until they came to Lake Patzcuaro, about whose shores lived the ancestors of the Tarascans. They were sedentary people who lived by planting crops in the lush wet lands by the lake and by fishing in its blue, sparkling waters. In all probability there was a grand fight down there by the lake shores; but they finally patched up the quarrel and the tribe from the hills of Zacapu settled down. Eventually they became the dominant faction of the merged tribe. Their story can best be told later on the shores of the lake where it happened.

Zacapu had turned out in gala dress to see the Gringos. The narrow, time-worn streets with their adobe houses were filled with children, school having been dismissed for the celebration. Hundreds of girls in Pablano costumes were lined up on both sides of the street. These Pablano costumes are something like the dairy-maids' costumes of comic opera — gay with ribbons. The Mexicans are a handsome people in any costume, and these children, with their black eyes and their olive skins, were adorable. They had baskets of confetti, but drew back from the temerity of throwing it. At last an old peasant woman asked me, with shy deprecation, 'Would you mind, señor, if the niñas threw confetti at you — in your honor?' I picked up the nearest little girl and kissed her. Then the battle began until the streets were like snow. At last we got to the top of the street under the blockhouse. A committee of prominent citizens — agitated almost beyond human endurance — began setting off sky-rockets. Being broad noon daylight, nobody could see the rockets, but the z-z-z-z-z of the whizzing stick seemed to supply a distinguished and impressive note.

The entire population of the town gathered around the door of the mayor's palace where we dined. They peered over each other's shoulders as they crowded about the windows and doors. When the street behind became so black and blocked with people that no one could move forward or backward, the front row obligingly sent bulletins back over their shoulders — relating the progress of our eating.

Our Spanish being a little weak, the one person at the feast who could speak English naturally absorbed the attention and the center of the stage. He was a flamboyant young man with a country barber-shop haircut — plastered back with great elegance on the starboard side. He had a bright red tie and a stick-pin made in the shape of a horseshoe. He said that he had been in the United States Navy; had served as steward on a trans-Atlantic liner sailing from New York, and now was foreman in a steel foundry in Cleveland, Ohio. He had come home to Zacapu to visit his father and mother, and was in great alarm for fear the new immigration laws of the United States would not allow him to return to his wife and baby. He said with great pride that his wife was an American girl and had blonde hair.

'If you can't go back to Cleveland, you could bring your wife and baby to Zacapu,' I suggested.

He was quite shocked. 'I couldn't do that — my wife, she is an artist.'

'What kind of an artist?'

'Well, once in a while, she and her partner get a job singing and dancing in the prologue at the movie theaters.'

'She has a partner?'

'Sure; yes.' Then, in answer to what seemed to be an unspoken question, he carefully produced a letter from his inside pocket. He read it aloud; then he asked me to read it aloud; then he translated it to the mayor, who sat in uncomfortable silence at the head of the table, wondering what it was all about. Then he handed the letter down the length of the table from hand to hand. The letter was written in a weak, scrawling hand, and this is what it said:

'Dear Husband: I love you, I adore you. I am well. The baby is well. I am dancing at the theater. Yours truly, Your Wife.'

After we had all read, seen and felt the letter, he took it back and read it aloud again.

At sunset that night, we stopped at the summit of a hill and watched the last rays flaming into the waters of Lake Patzcuaro. This mysterious lake is as beautiful as Tahoe and not as cold or as gloomy. The forest comes down to the shore. There are little islands that one can believe are enchanted. Descendants of the fisher people who were there in the lost ages are still running their log canoes into the rushes of the little lagoons. Across the face of the waters we could see the ancient capital of Tzintzunzan standing white against the mountains. It was the seat of the last emperor of the Tarascans. His name was Calzanzin. It was a fierce and haughty Indian federation which, to the end, defied Montezuma of the Aztecs.

Patzcuaro has always been an abode of the gods. When the invaders came from the hills of Zacapu, they brought with them a god of the hunting people — Taras. The lake people not only stole him bodily, but adopted his name.

There was also a goddess who had much to do with the coming of the rain. Back along the road, near a lonely Mexican village, we had stopped the cars to walk out into a field that was alive and bubbling with hot sulphur springs. The goddess was accustomed to snatch up victims from the fields and fishing-boats; cut out their living hearts, which she tossed into these boiling springs. By some alchemy known only to goddesses, these boiled hearts gave forth a steam that became rain-clouds.

There was also Tlaloc, who was a god of the lake, but who was apparently kidnapped to become one of the most important gods of the Aztecs. He became the third sun who re-created mankind — after a couple of cataclysms — only to see his work destroyed in a mighty fire that swept away all human beings.

When the planet Venus comes up over the hills of Patzcuaro, she looks like a flaming ball of fire — threatening and terrible. It is easy to believe that she was once among the great goddesses of the lake people at Patzcuaro.

Human history picks up this strange and self-reliant people about the time that the era of the Toltecs was drawing to a close — as they were slipping away for some unaccountable reason, leaving a pre-Aztec people to wander in from the hills to look in wonderment at the ruins of their beautiful civilization.

It was late that night when we saw the spires of Morelia, standing in a sparkle of light on a high plateau in the distance, a sparkle of lights against the thick black tropical darkness.

CHAPTER XXIV

SPOTLESS TOWN

MORELIA — the capital of Michoacan — is suggestive of nothing so much as an old New England house that has been made over by an architect — with the old doors and fireplace, but with hot and cold water and a telephone.

What has happened to Morelia is what will happen to all Mexico — modern sanitary regulations planned by young university men sitting in offices where heretics were tortured by the Inquisition; modern asphalt pavements carrying automobiles that whizz by the monastery where the Priest-General Morelos dropped his prayer-book for a sword.

Morelia is the cleanest city I have ever seen. It is absolutely spotless. It has one long magnificent street which once seen will be never forgotten. Upon this street are the cathedral, the Governor's palace, the college where the priest Morelos planned the Revolution against Spain, and another bishop's palace that is now a hotel.

The cathedral is, next to the cathedral in Pueblo, the finest church in Mexico, immeasurably finer architecturally than the famous cathedral in Mexico City. The latter has a regal magnificence of detail in its various chapels, but is too scattered and too diffused. It lacks a central motif. The cathedral in Morelia is not so large and not so magnificent, but it has cohesion and focus. You know where to look. It has composition. The cathedral in

Mexico City suggests a religion exposition — an art collection. The cathedral in Morelia fairly envelops and overwhelms you with its atmosphere.

Our hotel had been the palace of a bishop and was a place of faded magnificence with great patios with porticoes, with impressive alcoves outside the bedrooms. I had a room so large that one was fairly lost. The windows looked upon the majestic front of the cathedral and the chime of its great bells filled the room. The stairways fascinated me. They started and ended in extraordinary places, old half-dark recesses, rooms slipping into rooms. In the bishop's day it must have been a regal establishment with great retinues of servants.

The night of our arrival, the Governor of the State of Michoacan came to the hotel to meet us, and we had quite a gay and friendly time and we thought that from now on we knew him. But we discovered that to meet a Mexican Governor is no such light and frivolous matter. We had just spent an evening with him. We had not met him yet. Early the next morning, an aide in uniform arrived at the hotel to inform us that the Governor would receive us at the palace. We advanced on the place in state, driving our cars in through the great medieval gates into the open courtyard of what had been the seat of an archbishop. It was a grand palace built with huge balconies around a cobblestoned court.

It was like all government offices — stenographer girls finding business-like excuses to come out to look us over, aides scurrying in and out of offices. We were escorted in state to a reception-room. Finally, a great old door of the Middle Ages was thrown open and we were shown into a magnificent room with a blood-red carpet on the floor.

MORELIA, THE SPOTLESS TOWN

We were seated in a solemn row of chairs. Our merry, affable young friend of the night before — the Governor — sat there facing us. His face was frozen with solemnity. He said that he was honored by our coming. We said we were honored by his honor — the same 'line' as at the Governor's palace in Guadalajara. We sat there for some time. We were utterly miserable. He was miserable. At length we were aware that we might take our leave and rose stiff and solemn and august in our dignity. After we had departed with stiff and formal bows, we went down to the courtyard. Presently the Governor — now human again — came down also, and we talked about automobiles and tires and roads in the manner of the jolly little visit at the hotel the night before.

That afternoon he gave us a luncheon at a charming casino on the edge of town. It was a pleasant affair until we came to the speeches — when we froze into solemnity and dignity again.

A Mexican banquet is a pretty awful affair, although the speeches are far superior to the average of our American banquets. They are mercifully free from jokes about Scotchmen. They have vehemence and glow. I found a short way and a sure way to attain immortal fame as an orator. Called on to speak, I replied in English, and my remarks were much like a movie young lady speaking into the radio 'mike' on the night of a grand Hollywood movie opening. I am sure that every one has heard them... 'Hello, everybody. I am very glad to be here tonight and I am sure we are going to see a WON-derful WONderful picture. Good-bye, everybody.' That sounds very much like my remarks at Morelia. I must have said about thirty-five words, and they were not my very best words.

When I sat down, a young man at the other end of the table rose to translate my thoughts into Spanish.

'I cannot hope,' he said, 'to repeat in my poor way the golden eloquence, the glowing thoughts, the beautiful and poetic imagery with which Señor Carr has spoken.' Whereupon he translated my remarks for the next forty-five minutes and sat down amid a fury of enthusiastic applause. I was 'made' as an orator in that moment from the jungles of Yucatan to the jagged peaks of Sonora.

When I rose to speak, they, as usual, played the 'Diana' with a great flourish — 'Toot doodle de toot toot toot too.' I was reassured to learn that, in addition to playing it when the bull comes in, they also play it in token of great military victories. I am not sure whether I was a military victory or the début of the toro — but I guess it was all right. Anyhow, I was golden eloquence.

The Governor of Michoacan at that time was a young man named Lázaro Cardenas, one of Mexico's men of destiny — shy, simple, unaffected, and in terrible earnest. He had surrounded himself with an extraordinary group of young men — engineers — charming young university men. They have made a model city out of Morelia.

General Cardenas is, however, a devout adherent of the Agrarian Party and has filled the rich hacendados of Michoacan with indignation and alarm. He has an almost pathetic eagerness for recognition of his so-little-known state by Americans. He realizes that its future prosperity must depend upon publicity and tourists to a great extent. As the only newspaper man in the party, I was a strategic point. At the banquet he asked me with some evident anxiety what I thought of the State of Michoacan. There could not be room for two opinions about a state with one beautiful lake after another in a country of sublime mountains, with fields of golden wheat and fine horses. So my honest answer was one of admiration. That night he sent an aide to inquire of our party what I said about Michoacan in private conversation. Later, when we were received by the President of Mexico, who is a native of Michoacan, the procedure was repeated, with the additional question as to what I thought of General Cardenas.

The next day, the Governor sent an aide to show us the city. Especially his schools and hospitals. The most interesting of these is an industrial school for boys in an old Jesuit monastery of the Inquisition. The boys of this school are mostly waifs — some from the streets, some the orphaned sons of soldiers of the Revolution. It is a school of which any city might be proud. They are taught every kind of craft, from printing to repairing airplanes. It will be a surprise to my readers to know that Mexicans take to machinery like the proverbial duck to water. They are natural automobile mechanics. One of the features of the education of these boys is to conquer fear. They are taught never to acknowledge being afraid of anything. The monastery where they are in school is an interesting old place with an old torture-chamber and cells where the heretics were disciplined during the Inquisition, which was a very lively affair in Mexico. Old racks and the other machinery of agony and anguish have been removed from the ancient torture-chamber. It has been turned into a gymnasium. In Mexico, for some reason, it embarrasses them quite obviously when a visitor becomes too much interested in the events of the Inquisition. They are a super-sensitive and very 'touchy' people.

I know of no other place in Mexico where progress is in

such visible or dramatic terms as in Morelia. We went to
what had been the ruin of an old church. It is now a public library with more charm and atmosphere — because
of its peculiar construction — than others I have seen.

General Cardenas, among other reforms, was fighting
the drink habit among the peons. There were not many
cantinas in the city. On the walls of each saloon was, by
edict, a huge cartoon in color, depicting the evils of strong
drink. It strongly suggested our own W.C.T.U. warnings
of pre-Prohibition days. It had the same — 'Father, Oh,
Father, Come Home With Me Now,' motif; the degrada-
tion of the man who imbibes; the beaming happiness of the
virtuous man who forswears the demon Rum.

I called the attention of the polite little bartender in one
saloon to the dreadful warning. 'Es esta verdad?' I asked
him. (Is this true?) 'Es la ley.' (It is the law,) he replied
diplomatically, with a shrug of his shoulders.

The state lottery of Michoacan is conducted by an
American. The Mexican has an entirely different attitude
toward the lottery from ours. It is not only respectable:
it has acquired a certain distinction. The lottery is located
in a charming old building. It has its own printing-plant
and executive offices. The drawings take place in a sort of
patio. As showing how respectable people feel toward
lotteries, the director gave a ball in our honor and it was
attended by the élite of the city. The dancing took place
in the patio of the official weekly drawings.

To see Morelia without seeing the old college where the
Priest-General prepared the revolt against the imperial
power of Spain would be like going to Niagara without
looking at the Falls. Mexico is a country whose history
has been one long terrific drama, and the dramas that we

know have been built in the ashes of forgotten dramas that we know must have occurred before history began to be written. The West Coast of Mexico is redolent with romances, with high adventure, the footprints of gay young blades sallying forth, of Arab war-horses in search of the end of the rainbow. The Valley of Mexico to the south is scarred with the crash of battles and the débris of falling empires, of slaughtered Aztec kings and the bloodstains of human sacrifice. In these mountains, you are ever reminded of the struggle of Mexico for its freedom from Spain. The monastery where Morelos lived; the bridge where Hildalgo was beaten; marks of a struggle of simple Indian peasants armed with knives and clubs against the trained and tried troops of an imperial army.

CHAPTER XXV

THE MYSTERIOUS MOUNTAINS

WE LEFT Morelia in high state, with General Cardenas and his staff escorting us out to a crossroads where we met two cars of our party who had taken another route from Guadalajara — by way of Leon and Guanajuato.

They were bursting with exciting stories about their trip — of the great theater of Guanajuato: of the underground crypt where bodies mummified by some peculiar chemical quality of the soil stand propped up in rows waiting patiently for Judgment Day. Upon the faces of some of the mummies are expressions of horror and agony which suggested that they had been buried alive — in the days before modern embalming, a great many poor wretches unquestionably were. They told us of the street that was paved with silver to celebrate the wedding of the daughter of a Crœsus; of a tunnel made for street-cars which is being picked and pock-marked for the silver ore in the rock roofs and sides.

Our road went into a mountain country — and it requires considerable imagination and etiquette to call it a road. As we approached the mountain town of Ciudad Hidalgo, named for another priest-general of the Revolution, we saw a car waiting by the roadside: Into the middle of the road came three adorable little children dressed in Pablano costume, who flagged us down. They were Señorita Maria de la Luz Montoya, aged five, and Señorita Teresa de la Piña, aged seven. There was also a little boy, but, as is the usual fate of males, nobody paid much attention to him. A committee of grown-ups had also come out with speeches that they never had a chance to deliver. These two little girls with their black eyes captured the works. We made them ride with us as we rolled through streets that were snowing confetti, between lines of school-children. They were in charge of two beautiful young school-teachers.

I may seem to overwork the word 'beautiful,' but it is a temptation. I verily believe that the Mexicans are the handsomest race who inhabit the earth. Their erect pride of bearing, their grace and charm, their regular features, and those deep, glowing eyes are a study in human beauty. Their eyes have peculiar quality. They seem at once to be wet and hot. There is a damp, mysterious glow that seems to shut up the soul like a curtain, yet to suggest burning potentialities behind.

A luncheon banquet had been set for us under the trees behind an old house. We wrecked all their careful arrangements by insisting that the Señorita Teresa de la Piña should sit at the head of the table, which honor she filled with the serene and slightly bored composure of an empress presiding over a regiment of which she was honorary colonel.

It goes without saying that someone would have to perpetrate the usual feeble joke about going to the United States, to leave her father and mother, and be our little girl. An American child would have giggled. The Señorita Teresa lifted her eyes from her enchilada for a moment, looked the jester over from head to foot with calm, contemplative eyes; then said simply, 'No, thank you.'

That little banquet was a touching incident. We knew

that this village was almost starvation poor, yet they lavished the board with the choicest food their imaginations could conjure up. The *pièce de résistance* was young goat's meat, but there was every other kind of native food I ever heard of and many of which I had never heard. There was one especially delicious — something like the inside of a tamale served in an earthen jar. Peasant women hovered about the long table with great pitchers of pulque, which pale liquid is disturbing to the head, but soothing to the stomach and a good digestive agent.

They had the usual village orchestra — but this time with an added attraction. Some of the magnates of the town fairly dragged a bashful young peon in white cotton drawers and a cotton shirt up to the table. He was Fernando Delgado and he had composed a song. A comrade with a sunburned old guitar played the accompaniment while Fernando sang it for us. He was so shy that as he sang he kept his eyes on the trees with the fixed attention of a child looking at the chandeliers while speaking a piece on Friday afternoon.

Fernando sang his song, slipped back into the crowd, and was gone. I dare say he is down there somewhere in the mysterious mountains driving a burro — a genius who will never be heard of. If he were in the United States, he would probably be a famous song-writer of Tin-Pan Alley — on his way to Reno for a new and expensive divorce, riding in his Rolls-Royce with a retinue of servants who snicker at him. As it is, he is condemned to obscurity and peace of mind.

The song that he sang will be important source material for historians some day. The corrido is the voice from the dark stream of the native life of Mexico. It is to the peon what the saga was to the Nordic — the ballade to the early French.

Mexico is moving forward through a period of remarkable changes. These corridos will remain as the record of the emotion of a people. They compose a record more accurate — as registering a phase — than all the books written. There isn't much tune to them — a monotonous recitative with a certain pleasing lilt.

One well-known corrido, for instance, is *Las Esperanzas de la Patria por la Rendicion de Villa* (The hope of the country is for the surrender of Villa). Another, *La Toma de Zacatecas* (The Fall of Zacatecas). Another: *El Tren Descarrilado* (The train that jumped the track). *Triste Depedida de Emiliano Zapata* (The sad farewell of Zapata). The theme of most of these songs is, 'We are tired of fighting and we want to go home.'

There are many corridos of a later vintage; one tells of a Mexican peon who decided to go to Hollywood and become a famous movie star like Ramon Novarro. After many adventures, he wound up as a section hand on a railroad.

Fernando's corrido related the coming of the first airplane — a priceless historic record of the reactions of a primitive but humorous people. He told what the different villages of the neighborhood thought of this winged monster. This gave him an opportunity for sly digs — none of which he missed. It was witty, satirical, and delightful. It had a certain flavor you will find in the songs of no other people. Behind his inscrutable mask, the Mexican peon is a past-master of the delicate art of ridicule.

We stayed that night in a dreary little town. The hotel

was built like a prison with rows of bedrooms like cells looking out onto a balcony that looked down upon a narrow, cheerless patio. When we left that morning, we saw the peasant women going to early Mass — little shabby figures slipping through magnificent old doorways; the music of the solemn Mass; the same music that was being sung in great cathedrals of distant lands with the same imperial grandeur of candle and gold-crusted robes — and the realization was brought to me of what religion brings into the lives of these sad peons. To the women especially it is their life and their refuge. At the breakfast-table that morning we found the table adorned by a splendid bouquet of roses in an old jar of Mexican pottery and the simple card — 'Greetings from an American woman who lives in Zitacuaro.' We never heard more of her.

The roads from Zitacuaro climb straight up the mountains. The grades were severe. They called for everything that a car could muster. And frequently for something that they couldn't. The professional drivers made the grade. The one manned by an amateur driver stuck. Along came two peons with an old ox-cart and two lusty bueyos (oxen). Our colonel ordered them to unhitch and drag the car up. They cheerfully obeyed. They twisted ox-tails; put their own shoulders to the wheel, and yelled and struggled, and at last smiled benignly when the car snorted up the hill. The peons were so poor that the guarachas of one were only a couple of tattered shreds under his feet. Yet they looked astonished when one of our engineers held out a couple of pesos to them. They had no thought of pay. They had at last to be pressed to accept the money and went away fingering it in wonderment and embarrassment. There is a generous soul underneath the cotton shirts of these Mexican peons — until he gets into the hands of the labor agitators and is convinced that he is outraged and that his liberty has been undermined.

We climbed nearly ten thousand feet until our lungs panted with effort from the altitude when we walked up the steep slopes to lighten the struggling cars.

At last we came to an old town called San Bartolo which was altogether delightful — the city hall was an old building which appeared to have been born during the Middle Ages, with a cobblestoned court, narrow, hilly streets with the horses of the caballeros tied to old-fashioned hitching-racks like our early Dodge City towns. We stopped there to ask the mayor to send out oxen to the relief of the heavier cars which were trying to follow us.

The horses, in a way, establish the character of the peons in these mountains. They are a horse people. On the West Coast, you seldom see a peon on a horse; he rides burros. From generations of picking a precarious existence in a cruel, rainless country, the horses of the north of Mexico have acquired coarse hard mouths, pot-bellies, and fighting hearts. Feeding in herds has taken away their speed. The horses of these well-watered mountain valleys have always fed well. From time to time they have been improved by new blood. As a result, it is not unusal to see a peon riding on a magnificent charger that looks as though he had come from a horse show. Some of the finest horse-breeding farms in the world are in this part of Mexico. The revolutions have taken toll of them, however. In the last kick-up, there were troops of cavalry mounted on chargers that would have done credit to plumed knights.

Whenever we traveled on Sunday, we were pretty sure

to run into a horse-race, run on the open road behind
long lanes of mounted vaqueros. The grandstand is always
the back of a horse. I knew a man who had broken his leg
and insisted on being carried out to the back of his favorite
every morning while it was setting. He couldn't find any
other kind of chair that seemed comfortable to him.

On the long slope of a mountain road we met a touring-
car from which climbed one of the most remarkable men
in Mexico. We were to see much of him afterward in his
own State of Mexico, in Toluca, his capital, and afterward in the United States — Governor Filiberto Gomez.
With him had come to meet us two or three charming
young officers of his staff.

CHAPTER XXVI

YE OF SIMPLE FAITH

PEASANT life in these mountain towns of Michoacan is naïve and unspoiled. From our material viewpoint the peon doesn't get much out of life; but he puts untold sweetness into life.

Everything is an excuse to him for a fiesta. And every fiesta is a prayer. No doubt this is a subconscious reaching-back to his Indian blood. In some of the larger Mexican cities, the children look forward to some benign personage approximating our Santa Claus; but these little mountain children never heard of Saint Nick. They have a Christmas of their own, even more charming than ours.

The Mexican Christmas begins nine nights before Christmas Eve. Nine houses have been previously selected where the festivities are to occur. At seven o'clock in the evening, a procession starts, probably in a plaza or in the courtyard of some house that has been selected as a rendezvous. It is led by an old man recognized for his piety and social prestige. Walking with him at the front are usually two young girls who carry images of Saint Joseph and the Virgin Mary and often an image of the donkey upon which Mary rode — the burrito. Chanting the Christmas alavanzas — the special hymns of this occasion — they make their way down the street until they come to the house which is first to be host. Knocking at the door, the leader of the party asks for admission. 'Quien viene allí?' (Who is there?) comes the brusque lighted by the Star of Bethlehem, came bringing adoration and presents to the manger. In Mexico, they speak of the three wise men as the three kings, and this ceremony is called *Santos Reyes* (Holy Kings).

After the religious ceremonies, the host produces an enormous cake called the *Rosca*. It is something like a giant doughnut baked from cake flour. In the Rosca has been hidden a ring. If the family is wealthy, the ring is sometimes a beautiful gem. In poor families it is sometimes a simple toy. Wealth or the lack of it is a matter of unembarrassed frankness in Mexico. The guests in turn cut the cake and one, of course, gets the ring. These guests are always those who were present at the Christmas ceremonies. Winning the ring by a lucky cut is not an unmixed blessing. It involves the obligation to become host at 'El Dia de Candelaria' (The Day of the Candle).

On the night of Santos Reyes, all the children must go to bed promptly at nine o'clock and you can be sure no niña begs off on this wonderful night. As they go to bed, they leave their little shoes on the sills of their windows. In the night the camels which composed the caravan of the three wise men go pad-pad-padding along the roads and streets and the little shoes are filled with gifts from their packs — just as American children are visited by the reindeer of Santa Claus.

The Day of the Candles is supposed to be the anniversary of the day when Mary took her infant son to the Temple. In Mexico, it is the day when the seeds are blessed. Each little rancherito with simple faith brings one tenth of his last year's crop as a present to the Church and his saints. Also he brings the seed to be planted in the coming season. The peon is always a little inclined to bargain with his saints. If the saint blesses the seed with fertility, then his one-tenth tithing on the next Candle Day will be so much the larger. After the religious ceremonies the peons spend the day exchanging seeds with one another to strengthen their crops. And of course they dance. The Day of the Candle is February 2.

One of the sweetest and most affecting sights in the world is a Mexican pueblo in Mes de Maria, the month of Mary. Every day from May 1 to May 31, flowers are brought to the Virgin. Each day of that month the church is turned over to a different family for decoration. Often this involves the idea of penitence and gratitude. If a Mexican family has grave illness or dire trouble, it is usual to promise the Virgin to bring her flowers on a day in May if she will help them in their affliction by her prayers.

The family whose day it is to decorate the church makes elaborate preparations long in advance. In the case of well-to-do families, orders have been placed with florists for white blossoms. The flowers, in any event, must always be white. In the case of poorer families, they find wild flowers or even make paper flowers, which the Mexicans do with extraordinary artistry.

The flowers are placed in the vestibule of the church in readiness for a procession of little girls — all in white and wearing tiny wedding veils on their heads. As they come into the vestibule of the church, singing hymns, each is handed a basket or a bouquet of flowers. They march into the church and the ceremony of singing the Rosary begins. After 'Hail, Mary,' has been sung for the tenth time, two or more of the little brides walk up the main aisle and lay their white flowers at the feet of the Virgin. Ten more 'Hail, Marys'; then more little girls marching was near, he rang the famous Mexican Liberty Bell at eleven o'clock on the night of the 16th. The historic fact seems to be that he was informed by a secret messenger at two o'clock on the morning of September 16, and at early Mass made the stirring appeal that has ever since been known as 'Grito de Dolores' — the cry of Dolores. The evening of Independence Day is known to the peons as 'Noche del Grito' — night of the war-cry. In Mexico City, the President of the Republic comes to the balcony of the palacio at eleven o'clock; strikes the Liberty Bell which has been preserved in the National Museum and cries 'Viva La Independencia.' It is the dramatic climax to what is possibly the most dramatic patriotic celebration on the American continent.

Benito Juarez, Miguel Hidalgo y Costilla, and José María Morelos, in Mexico, are names like Washington and Lincoln and Grant with us.

The two latter heroes are venerated as martyrs. Both Hidalgo and Morelos were executed by the Spanish and their heads impaled in public for eleven days.

The Mexican finds nothing whatever incongruous in interrupting the lovely and touching ceremony of the Mes de Maria, with its prayers and white flowers, to whoop and shoot firecrackers in memory of Don Benito — and why should he?

And just so, why should he not come home from the solemn and sacred Mass of the Birth of Jesus and dance the night out. The God of the peon does not demand solemn faces.

CHAPTER XXVII

THE BEAUTIFUL CITY

MEXICAN cities have character. They are like people.

Hermosillo is an elegant ranchero mounted on a splendid Palomino horse.

Guaymas is a lovely, sad, aristocratic old señora in a faded mantilla.

Mazatlan is an orchid growing in a smelly old patio.

Tepic, an ancient aristocrat sipping his aguardiente in his courtyard while his orchestra plays.

Guadalajara, a cynical young Spanish cavalier with a light guitar, serenading a girl he has never seen — to win a bet.

Morelia, a shining Rolls-Royce dragging an ox-cart.

Ciudad de Mexico — the City of Mexico — an Aztec princess of merciless beauty dressed in a Paris gown, stepping with delicate disdain across pools of blood shed by men who fought over her. Ciudad de Mexico is Paris; it is Berlin; it is an ancient Aztec capital; it is Hollywood. It is every city.

Every one has his own Mexico City. There is a Mexico City with nothing in it but dim old libraries, containing manuscripts written in the regal flourishes of the Spanish authors of the days of chivalry. There is a Mexico City that contains nothing but the footprints and blood stains of history. Another Mexico City has only mystery — the whispering ghosts of old religions, ancient rites, and forgotten philosophies. Yet another Mexico City is entirely

a city of beautiful works of art — beautiful buildings,
superb statues, stark, wonderful paintings, murals that
overwhelm you with their crude, wild strength. There is
again a Mexico City that lives like a beautiful flower of
the night — dark-eyed señoritas and sensuous music and
laughter and flowers.

My Mexico City is a stage — a stage where mighty
dramas have been played; where strong men have fought
for power and died in their armor. There is no other city
in the world — unless it be Imperial Rome — where so
much history has been written; so much blood spilled.

The city presents a picture of sharp and thrilling beauty.
Through its heart runs one of the most magnificent boulevards in the world. At one end is Chapultepec Castle;
at the other end, the Palacio and the great cathedral —
waterlogged with drama and history. Through the mists
the snow-peaks of Popocatepetl and Iztaccihuatl are
dimly seen like ghost mountains. Although it lies in a
long level valley, Ciudad Mexico is very high — between
seven thousand and eight thousand feet — and the thin
air sparkles and snaps with vitality.

It is Mexico, but not Mexico of the rebosos and the
tortillas. You are conscious of the native life only as a
dark stream running silently below the surface. You
may perhaps dine in a café that was an old monastery
scarred by the swords of Cortes and with Aztec graves
beneath its foundation stones; but you dine with a Paris
gown and a malacca stick. That it should be a cosmo-
politan city is natural when you remember who built it —
ancient and long-forgotten Toltec craftsmen — Montezuma, Cortes, and the Empress Carlotta of Austria.

The hotel lobbies reminded me of The Hague during

the World War — well-dressed gentlemen of mystery and without visible means of support, whispering to you of their intimate connections with powerful persons. In Mexico they are called *coyotes*. Fine automobiles drawing up at the hotel doors; fashionable women making their way through the dark river of Mexican life on the sidewalks; peons with loads on their heads; insistent street beggars; peddlers of blankets; dulce-sellers, postcard merchants; abashed, silent women in rebosos — the dark stream.

To stroll around the streets is to acquire a never-ending succession of gooseflesh thrills. You stop to buy flowers at a little stand fronting a park, and it is suddenly borne in upon you that this street, with its solemn and respectable-looking office buildings, was the bloody Causeway where the Knights of Spain died on Noche Tríste — the Sad Night when so many Spanish families went into mourning. Somewhere in the middle of what is now an asphalt street full of rushing taxicabs was the place where Alvarado put the butt of his lance down upon the corpses and wreckage of the canal and saved his life by the first pole vault in the history of the world — a mighty leap in full armor — helped on considerably by the arrows and javelins of the yelling Aztec warriors.

You pass a somber old monastic-looking building in the old part of the city and realize that this is the College of San Fernando where Father Serra chanted his litanies before he started on his tremendous crusade to civilize the Indians of California and to establish the missions of Camino Real.

Another dark building in the old quarter was a monastery where a son of Cortes and the luscious Marina was tortured in the Inquisition. After nearly tearing him to pieces, the Spanish government sent him word that it was all a little mistake and he could consider himself innocent — which must have helped his broken body a lot.

As you stop to buy a carved leather cigarette-case on the Avenida Juarez, someone points out in the most casual way that the park right back of the shop was the place where the heretics were burned from time to time as a gentle suggestion to the pious.

The Cathedral and the Plaza Mayor and the Palacio are all drenched with memories of Montezuma. The Aztecs were not very old-timers in Mexico. They came in from the north about five hundred years before Cortes began the Conquest. It is a matter of historic experience that some of the most magnificent civilizations have resulted from the conquest of a sedentary, artistic people by a race of military invaders. The Aztecs had arrived as a subject people, but had fought their way to domination. Montezuma was in full flower when Cortes arrived. He was stepping high, wide, and handsome. His court was one of regal and incomparable splendor. Even his soldiers were arrayed with the gorgeousness of Oriental princes. The Aztec army must have been a grand sight with their cloaks of feathers and head-dresses sometimes of gold and silver.

Where the cathedral now stands was an Aztec temple built like a pyramid with terraces. At the top was the sacrificial stone upon which the victims were laid while the priest tore them open and ripped out their living hearts. Sometimes the victims were prisoners of war; but every year the priests sacrificed a beautiful boy. For a year they fed him on the fat of the land and allowed him to wander around the city enjoying himself. Although it occurs to me that the morning occupation of counting the days until his heart was to be cut out while a priest bent his back over a rock was not the best inspiration for a holiday. A month before he died, they always sent the beautiful boy four young wives — who no doubt were also beautiful. In the circumstances even this four-ply honeymoon must have had its drawbacks. These brides were supposed to stand around and watch his bloody death on the sacrificial stone and contribute their grief to the show.

This grim sacrificial stone is still in the Mexican Museum — along with various Aztec gods, Maximilian's carriage and Indian handwork and native crafts. Somehow the stone does not look sufficiently wicked. I was disappointed. Nothing looks dramatic in a museum.

The day I went through the museum I fell into the hands of a young professor from the University of Mexico. As we went around the exhibits, he suddenly stopped and said: 'Say, who are you anyhow?' 'A fellow going through a museum,' I replied meekly. 'Yes, but you are somebody different. Come on; let's start all over again.' So we started at the beginning again. He explained the great calendar stone and so many symbolisms that my head reeled. I felt like the Jewish gentleman who said to the professor of algebra, 'I don't know what you mean — I am just listening because I like to hear the numbers.'

I came out of the daze at least with this; that the calendar stone of the Aztecs was far more than a calendar; it is a religion in shorthand and perhaps the most amazing relic in the world. Superficially there isn't much mystery about the Aztecs. Their ceremonies are known in the most intricate detail; just so their gods and their philosophy. There is even in existence a letter from an Aztec mother to her flapper daughter that sounds like the Beatrice Fairfax column in the Hearst newspapers. In Mexico City there are several classes where the Aztec language is taught. It is a terrible language to see in print, but pleasant to the ear. Near Durango there is a village where pure Aztec is spoken. It sounds like the twitter of birds.

The Spaniards destroyed every vestige of the old temple to build the modern cathedral. Only a wall half excavated on a side street back of the church remains of the mighty Indian city of Tenochtitlan.

The cathedral is rather overwhelming. You can walk into any ordinary church; absorb what spiritual inspiration is there for you and walk out — having in a measure seen the church. To say you have seen the cathedral in Mexico City is about like saying you have seen the British Museum or that you know music. It is a place to study rather than to see. Its art treasures, its side chapels, its sacred images, its altars...It is an aggregation of many churches in one church. Its splendor and magnificence overawe the most casual visitor, but it is for artists and savants to appreciate it in detail.

Personally, it was an overdose for my cosmic consciousness. My favorite churches in all Mexico still remain the cathedral at Puebla, the cathedral at Morelia, and the little Church of Our Lady of Aranzazu in Guadalajara.

On one side of the Plaza Mayor, where the Palacio now stands, was an old Aztec palace. It is said to have been at this place that Montezuma, a prisoner of war, stood and tried to tell his people the Spaniards were his loving friends and that all was well. It is interesting to imagine what would have happened and how the history of the world might have been changed if Montezuma had had the courage to stand there on the balcony and yell out to his people a call to arms. That moment on the balcony of the ancient palace is one of the crucial moments of human history.

Montezuma was a weak voluptuary. The Aztec Empire groaned under the weight of his tyranny. When he dined in royal state, three hundred subjects waited on him. More than a hundred viands were always placed before him. He pointed the golden royal scepter at what he wished to eat. No one addressed him without making three bows and exclaiming, 'Lord, my Lord, Great Lord,' without raising the eyes. The slightest carelessness of a servant meant death by torture. In fact, he suggested the imperious stupendousness of a Hollywood movie director, and the gorgeousness of his surroundings at times approached the elegance of a Cecil De Mille movie set, although, of course, I don't know about the bathrooms... When Cortes arrived with his war-horses and his cannon, the bold Montezuma collapsed like a bank check marked 'no funds.'

Had he come out that day to the balcony with a call to arms, the Spanish army would probably have been destroyed. Cortes was in a bad way. He had only a handful of men; he had been disowned by the Spanish Government. As it was, when the Emperor came out to the balcony — dressed as usual in his best clothes — the noble young Cuahutemoc heaved a brick at him. The Spanish announced that the blow had killed him; but doubtless he received what the police of today call 'special treatment' after they got him back into the house. Anyhow, he died and the Spanish — in the confusion — managed to escape in the night down that bloodstained causeway. Cuahutemoc took command of his people, but was finally captured and tortured to death. A fine statue of this gallant young fellow now stands in the middle of the Avenida Reforma below Chapultepec.

Bad as Montezuma was, the Spanish Conquistadores were worse. Compared with the record of Cortes and Alvarado, Al Capone is a fragrant white lily. There was no treachery of which they were not guilty. The war with the Aztecs was started, probably in this same historic square in front of the cathedral, while the natives were giving a fiesta in honor of Alvarado. In the middle of the dance, Alvarado's soldiers leaped into the audience with swords and cut them to pieces.

Fronting on the far side of the Plaza Mayor, the Aztecs had a great market where they sold everything, from native jewelry and corn to slaves with collars around their necks. Back of this market now stands the Thieves' Market. I have heard many tourists and Mexican residents tell of buying priceless treasures for a song in this place. Many residents used to go there to buy back their own stolen property. I saw nothing there but junk. It looked like a cross between a country fair and a five-and-ten-cent store. I was looking for swords of Spanish chivalry. I found Mexican shoes, old stoves, and cheap tinware. The Thieves' Market has been condemned for a new court house. A much more entertaining place is the national pawnshop, where from time to time pledged articles are auctioned off. Bargains. This also is near the Zocolo.

Here and there in the city you come across scars of the American invasion — what we call the 'Mexican War'— which brought California, Arizona, New Mexico, and Texas into the Union. General Grant, as a young officer, is said to have been quartered in the Palacio. Military experts of our own army tell me that the American victory was due to the mercy of High Heaven. General Scott, who was not overweighted with brains, is said to have committed a military absurdity and would have been licked to a finish except for a quarrel between two Mexican generals who could not agree upon a plan. So, as to the American occupation, it is safer to say, with the Two Black Crows, 'Why bring that up?'

One of the most interesting places in Mexico is the long row of little shops — really open booths — which line the edges of the Alameda. Sometimes they run clear around the edges of the park. On Sundays they make a great country fair; on Monday, two thirds of them have disappeared. In Jalisco one finds pottery; in Mazatlan, iguana shoes; in Pueblo, blankets. But here you find them all — the pottery of Jalisco, the iguana shoes of Mazatlan, and blankets of Pueblo.

Here is a little booth where old Juan makes his little pottery figures. With a thimbleful of clay, a little wire and thread, he will turn out a charging bull or a vaquero mounted on a rearing pony or a matador with the espada poised against the bull. The head of the vaquero may be no larger than a match, but his features are all there. Pleased with your praise, old Juan will shrug his shoulders and murmur, 'Es nada; mira.' And he shows you half of

a peanut shell in which there is moulded a woodland scene.
Under the glass it shows completeness in every little detail. Yet old Juan wouldn't know what to do with a glass.
He comes from a people with eyes — the Jalisco Indians.
Some of these Indians have been known to make an accurate count of cattle so far away that to Gringo eyes
they were only a faint cloud of dust in the distance.

Here is a booth where a shy little Mexican sells dressed
up fleas. Under a magnifying-glass we see that each
flea is dressed correctly in the complete attire of el toreador.
Old Concepcion, withered with age, sells guajes — gourds
— grown, shaped, and painted by the Tarascan Indians
of Michoacan — painted in scarlet and black and gold —
gourds that have been made into cups, pocketbooks,
plates, jugs, musical instruments, and art objects. The
lacquers and vivid paints are secrets — age old — of the
Tarascans. Some of the gourds are amazing. On the
vines they have been trained into alligators, egrets,
swans.

The next booth is also an art studio — mounted
vaqueros, bandits of ferocious appearance; little toys
made of tule grass by the military prisoners; José and his
beautiful colored candles from Durango; yellow candles
with green-and-red stripes. The art of dyeing these
candles has come down to him from long generations.
Maria, who makes tamales and enchiladas; Esteban, who
will carve a piece of cowhide into the most beautiful
revolver-holster or a cigarette-case while you stand there.
You can name your own design or he will carve into the
leather the Mexican coat-of-arms — the eagle perched on
a cactus branch strangling a snake. It was this eagle who
gave the signal to the nomadic Aztecs that they had ar-

rived at the Promised Land and their long wanderings
were at an end...the fulfillment of an old prophecy. I
have observed that these magical sign-posts, erected by
Providence for the guidance of various wandering peoples,
always seem to be on mighty good land that belongs to
somebody else. The eagles and the arrowheads and the
snakes are a strict command to the pious that it is their
solemn duty to grab it.

Blankets of scarlet and white, blankets of black and
gray; exquisite lace and drawn-work; silver filigree; chairs
with seats made of cowhide — the hair still on; chairs
made from mesquite and hide from the Yaqui country;
strange pottery from the Mayan country to the south,
made amid the ruins of lost cities; echoes from the myriad
lives of my sweet, gentle, fierce, patient, fire-eating old
Mother Mexico who dances gay fandangos on blood-
soaked ground.

CHAPTER XXVIII

CHAPULTEPEC

BREAKFAST... It is a long bar-room in the hotel. At one side is the polished bar; along the other side of the room are the booths, spotless with white tablecloths. We give our orders to the Mexican waiter and puzzle through the morning papers while we wait. In comes a party of newspaper men — a correspondent of a syndicate of American papers — and two charming Mexicans. One has an Irish name, but his people have been so long in Mexico that he speaks English with a strong native accent. We become conscious of another figure behind us, and there stands El Norteño, still walking gingerly in his stylish shoes with his collegiate hat balanced precariously on his head. Goodness knows where El Norteño stays; he has a hotel room somewhere among his own people.

A soldierly looking young officer comes up, who bows formally as he asks, 'Pardon me — were you not at Naco during the battles?' I return a surprised 'Why, yes.' And then at the bar, leaning on one elbow, I see my old compañero the General — the gay, reckless young general who got up at ten o'clock in the morning, battle or no battle. We give each other the embrazo with much patting on the back. Our breakfast party expands to the limit of the table; then on into the aisle...

One of our engineers leans over and whispers... 'Today's the day. Hurry through your breakfast and come.' We finish the huevos and coffee and excuse ourselves.

Today we are to be received by the President of Mexico at Chapultepec.

Celebrities are coming thick and fast. It was only yesterday that we were received by General Almazon in the big bleak office building where he holds forth as Minister of Communications. He is one of the strong men of Mexico, bulking large physically as well as mentally. I remembered him as he marched down from Pulpito Pass during the Revolution at the head of eight thousand of the best troops ever seen in Mexico.

I remembered his social adroitness at the American Club in Agua Prieta the night of his arrival. A brash American traveling man, seeing him sitting with an officer of his staff at a table, had called the waiter and said, 'Take a bottle of wine to that gentleman's table.' For just an instant the General looked dismayed at this social brashness. Then he turned to the waiter and said, 'Take a bottle of champagne to every table in the American Club.' The drummer should have been squelched, but I imagine he completely missed the rebuke.

And in the afternoon we had met General Amaro at the country club. He, too, is one of the most remarkable men in all Mexico. A full-blooded Indian, he is Secretary of War and a brilliant soldier. When he first came to the capital, he was a primitive. In two or three years he has mastered English, French, German, and Russian. When he first arrived, he wore one earring. Among his people this was not an ornament. The man who had killed his father still lived. In due course of time the earring disappeared. Draw your own conclusions.

And now we were to be received by Ortiz Rubio, President of Mexico. An officer of the presidential staff had a car waiting for us at the door. We rolled along the magnificent Avenida Reforma — past the monument to the liberators of Mexico, one of the finest works of art in any city of the world; past the monument to the memory of the martyred Aztec Chuahutemoc; past the American Embassy, into the depths of the great cypress forest above whose tops rear the terraces of Chapultepec. At one time the forest was a magnificent wild-animal park, but the officers of one of the revolutions gave a swell hunting party and killed them all. The road circles round the hill and at length we swept around into a graveled courtyard speckled with soldiers on guard — Chapultepec.

There are palaces in Europe that are peopled with memories; but they are new bungalows compared with Chapultepec and its ghosts. No one knows who first occupied the site. Before the Aztecs came into the Valley of Mexico, some forgotten king had his palace here. Montezuma had his summer place here with his harem when the Spanish came.

The foundations of the present castle were laid in 1783 by one of the Spanish viceroys. He laid himself out so elaborately in the way of house that all work was stopped for a time by order of the Spanish King. He thought the man must be building a fortress instead of a house, from the size of the bills. It was hammered to pieces by the cannon of the Yankees when Mexico City was captured during our Mexican War. Over here at the edge of the courtyard is a parapet looking down the side of a deep precipice into the cypress forest. With a deprecating smile, our guide explained that over this cliff two little cadets fourteen years old had thrown themselves to certain death rather than basely surrender to the Gringos;

CHAPULTEPEC

the defense of Chapultepec was largely in the hands of little boy cadets.

We were ushered into a small reception-room on the ground floor. Presently a young officer in a uniform that fitted like a glove came with word that the Presidente desired that we should be shown over the castle while we waited. It is a beautiful place. We stood on the great terrace and looked over the Valley of Mexico where history has been written in blood; over the lovely city that pours down the length of the valley like a world's fair in crystal white; out through the haze of the morning to the snow-peaks of old Popocatepetl and Iztaccihuatl; through vistas of brocaded and wainscoted rooms; into the coral-tinted bedroom and apartments of the Empress Carlotta; into the somber elegance of the imperial dining-room of the Emperor Maximilian.

The spirits of Carlotta and Maximilian pervade Chapultepec. It was she who planned the present castle out of the ruins left by the Gringo shells. She also who planned the modern City of Mexico with its broad boulevards. In her apartments with her regal bed and the rose-pink brocades, everything is as though she had just stepped out.

The tragedy of Maximilian is Chapultepec's best drama because it was a drama of women. It is one of the ironies of history that the innocent, well-meaning monarchs are the victims who have to 'take the rap.' The Peter the Greats and the blood-thirsty Ivans the Terribles die of indigestion. It is the meek, inoffensive little henpecked married men, like Nicholas and Maximilian, who are assassinated in dark Russian cellars and die in front of firing squads.

I have often wondered to what extent the history of the world would have been changed had the pulchritudinous Miss Maria Eugénie Ignace Augustiné de Montija de Guzman been cross-eyed or had had buck teeth and a mole on her nose. As it was, she was so beautiful that the fatuous Napoleon III married her and she became Empress Eugénie. Her insatiable lust for power wrecked the French Empire and brought a harmless Austrian archduke a peck of trouble.

It was a great story — a story of three women: Eugénie, who evolved the idea of a Mexican empire under the thumb of France. When the defeat of the Confederate army in the Civil War gummed up her conspiracy, she abandoned Maximilian to his fate. Carlotta, the beautiful Belgian consort of Maximilian, packed her suitcase and went back to France to take the French Emperor to task. Eugénie promptly threw a beautiful and well-planned swoon, and Napoleon blubbered and sniffled and said he couldn't do a darn thing. So the beautiful Carlotta's reason reeled. Through all the years until her death, three or four years ago, she sat in a Belgian château, still believing herself to be Empress of Mexico. Her marriage with Maximilian was a charming love-story. Her last message to him from Europe was heart-rending. Believing herself the object of a poison plot, she wrote him this message: 'Dearly beloved treasure: I bid you farewell. God is calling me to him. I thank you for the happiness which you have always given me. May God bless you and help you to win eternal bliss. Your faithful Carlotta.'

Another woman entered into this grim tragedy. She had shared the happy golden days of the last Empire.

It was a sort of play empire. The courtiers of Maximilian delighted to dress themselves up as Mexican caballeros galloping around the country with jingling spurs. Carlotta had a carriage drawn by six cream-colored mules — two at the pole and four abreast as leaders. One of those about the court was the Prince Salm Salm, a German soldier of fortune. He had married a beautiful French-American girl. It was court gossip that she had been a circus rider. The story of the Prince Salm Salm — and of the Princess — is one of desperate and romantic loyalty to a lost cause. When nearly all the others had deserted Maximilian, they stuck. In the last days — her husband in a military prison, Maximilian under sentence of death — the Princess tried to save the doomed man. According to a story left by an officer of the Emperor's staff, the Princess Salm Salm inveigled the commander of the death-watch into her rooms at Quaretaro. First, she offered him one hundred thousand pesos to allow the Emperor to escape. This being refused, she said: 'Is that not enough? Then here I am, Colonel.' And began to take off her clothes. It is related that the officer was so thoroughly alarmed at this Saint Anthony temptation that he tried to run out of the door; found it locked; threatened to jump out of the window unless she put on her clothes and let him out. The Princess Salm Salm then rode on horseback to the stern revolutionary chief, Benito Juarez, and knelt before him, clinging to his knees when he tried to raise her, begging for the life of Maximilian. He told her sadly that he could not spare the life of Maximilian if all the kings and queens of Europe were kneeling at his feet.

In Los Angeles I knew one of the officers of the firing squad who shot Maximilian to death on the 'Hill of the

Bells' at Queretaro. He was a Pole, Colonel John Sobieski, descendant of Poland's great Sobieski. He told me how the Emperor shook hands with each soldier; handed them each twenty dollars, and asked them to shoot straight. But each dreaded the job, so they haggled him. So Colonel Sobieski handed his revolver to the sergeant, who placed it to the ear of the wounded man and pulled the trigger. When I knew Colonel Sobieski, he was a temperance lecturer.

Ghosts of the tragedy of Maximilian — ghosts of the tragedies of Porfirio Diaz — of Madero — ghosts of Chapultepec...

In the little 'Yank-Mex' town of Los Mochis among the sugar-cane plantations I formed a firm friendship with one Colonel Octavio Serrano, who had been eyewitness to the tragedies of Diaz and Madero. As a little boy of twelve he had run away from his home in Guadalajara and had made his way to Mexico City, hiding under the car seats. He had resolved to be an army officer. Making his living like a sparrow on the streets, he came every day to the Palacio, there to wait all day long in the hope of meeting El Presidente. For three months he waited — with the patient endurance of his race. One day he fell asleep and an indignant hand jolted him awake. His sleepy eyes saw an officer of El Presidente's staff, reproaching him for using the President's waiting-room for a lodging-house. The little fellow faltered out his story. 'Hm, Hm,' temporized the officer. 'Come here tomorrow.' When he was at last ushered into the presence of the great Don Porfirio, he was so overcome that he could only burst into tears and cry, 'El Presidente, military school, military school!' Although under age, he was admitted by the President's order. When the sudden collapse of the Diaz régime came, he violated all military discipline and sent a personal telegram to the President, in which he said, 'I ask for the privilege of dying at your side.' Don Porfirio, deeply touched, told him to come on. Once at Chapultepec, he found to his dismay that Diaz had no realization of the tragedy. He thought it would blow over and everything would turn out all right.

When Madero came to Chapultepec, he retained Colonel Serrano as his aide in spite of his protestations of undying loyalty to Don Porfirio. The day that Madero was assassinated, all the members of his staff were put in prison. Colonel Serrano, giving his honor as a Mason to return, was allowed to go out to look after Mrs. Madero, who, of course, was in great danger. He put her in a carriage and sought refuge for her in one of the Embassies. She refused to be taken to the Embassy of the United States. In the bitterness of her heart she said she would rather die. The French Ambassador looked into vacancy and hemmed and hawed and well — really — you-see-how-it-is. At length in despair they went to the Japanese.

The Japanese Ambassador heard the plea, but made no answer. Instead he turned to a servant and gave a sharp order. Presently several servants came out bearing a strip of scarlet carpet which they spread from the front door to Mrs. Madero's carriage. As Colonel Serrano said farewell — as he had to go back to jail — the Japanese Ambassador said, with quiet dignity, 'If anything happens to this lady, you will know, in your jail cell, that our dead bodies are lying at her feet.'

Afterward, when Pancho Villa captured Zacatecas after a terrific battle in which men were killed at the rate of one thousand an hour, Colonel Serrano was captured and sentenced to death. He was saved by a telegraphic appeal to Villa from Mrs. Madero, then in the United States.

We were wafted back into the present day by the arrival of a young officer who announced that El Presidente was ready to receive us. Over a broad terrace we were brought into a beautiful reception-room that might have been a room of the Palace of Louis XVI. It was light, airy, and charming. On a grand piano stood a large photograph of Herbert Hoover. It was the only picture in the room.

The President of Mexico stood in the middle of the room waiting to receive us. Ortiz Rubio is a type of high official not often seen in Mexico. He is not a soldier, but an engineer and a very capable one. He is rather tall and well made, with a pleasant face. On this particular occasion a patch of surgical plaster disfigured one side of his face — the mark of a would-be assassin's bullet. I could not help observing that he took a chair alone with his back to the wall near a corner of the grand piano. We were seated in a semicircle in front of him. Our backs were toward two French doors that opened out onto the terrace. At each of these two doors lingered two young officers. I noticed that their trim uniforms bulged over the right hip and that they never took their eyes off our backs. A hostile movement on the part of any of us would have been a brief and economical method of suicide.

We talked through an interpreter, but I had a feeling that the President understood English as well as any of us. We had found General Almazon rather chilly and formal, but Ortiz Rubio was quite chatty and friendly. As an engineer he was deeply interested in the project of building the international highway we had scouted. He asked all kinds of questions. At length he turned to me, the only journalist present.

'His Excellency,' said the interpreter, 'wishes to know what Señor Carr thought of the State of Michoacan.' He beamed when I told him my impressions of that lovely mountain country, with its clean cities and its beautiful lakes.

'His Excellency' wishes to say to Señor Carr that he is deeply gratified to hear these impressions, as Michoacan is his home land.'

Somehow I got the heavenly inspiration to say that, although Michoacan was a beautiful country, I thought of it only as a setting for its great men — that its greatest product was its progressive, outstanding men, like General Cardenas, the Governor, and his staff of brilliant young experts.

The President smiled and nodded; then the interpreter added: 'His Excellency wishes to say that he is particularly gratified to know that you feel this way as he regards General Cardenas as one of the most promising men in all Mexico.'

CHAPTER XXIX
HISTORIC FOOTPRINTS

EVERY morning, through the courtesy of an old friend of mine, a limousine with a driver drew up in front of the hotel for our daily 'buggy ride.' Also — and this was unusual in a Latin country — came the daughter of the house to be our guide. She was eighteen — a very pretty girl. Educated in a California finishing school, she had returned to the cloistered life of a Mexican girl of the aristocracy; and she was perishing by inches of ennui. Like the women of her race, she was silent before the wishes of men, compliant, simpática. She had no desires beyond the pleasure of her guests and had very little to say. Unlike most American girls, she understood the intricacies of politics. One man at the hotel had told us, with the confidential whisper of the coyote, that his friend at the next table was to be the next Governor of Yucatan. He could provide an introduction — for a consideration.

'Don't bother with him,' she said quietly. 'He is the jefe of the garrison in a little Mexican State and he will never see Yucatan.' She knew the intrigues of this general and that...as she knew the location of the Hollywood studios; and she knew them like a postman.

One day we went to Xochimilco to see the famous floating gardens. This is just about the loveliest place in the whole world. Originally the gardens were planted on floating rafts of wicker; now they have taken root. To all intents and purposes, Xochimilco is a Venice of flower-boats. Whereas in Venice you gondola your way between gloomy, dank palaces, the canals of Xochimilco ramble through immense fields of blossoms. The boats upon which you ride are floating bowers of beauty and fragrance. Usually you hire a little string orchestra to play as you ride. Some of the boats have tables under a canopy where you dine to the strains of *Estrellita* in the perfume of flowers. As the boatman poles his way along, you pass market boats absolutely hidden by blossoms, so that the effect is of a floating bouquet. The sight of an Iowa farmer who has made a killing in pigs, floating along on this dolce far niente sea of perfume to the accompaniment of the soft thrum of guitars, gives an impression of dreamy elegance not to be forgotten.

Yet Xochimilco has had its battle scars, too. Some of the most savage of the early Aztec wars were against this tribe of blossom-sellers. And in the days of the Aztec Empire the feather-cloaked army was always uneasily waiting for the battle-cry which would announce that Xochimilco had jumped the reservation again. In those days the favorite blossom of the floating gardens must have been the tiger lily.

Often, in these days, we went for luncheon in the lovely old hotel at San Angel. The guides say that it was a convent, and it may have been used at some time by the nuns; but I saw an abstract of the real estate title and it showed that it was the casa of a great hacienda. At any rate, it is a charming place of quiet, dreamy old patios, ancient corridors, quaint old passages, terraces, and sacred shrines. It is hundreds of years old.

Another day we went to Coyoacan to see the little

church where Cortes went to say his prayers for Divine guidance on the job of killing and torturing the Aztecs, from whom he was planning to wrest their home lands and wreck their civilization — the Aztecs who had received him with open arms as an honored guest.

Cortes stands in history without parallel — either for treachery or military genius. He had the shining morals of a Chinese hatchetman; but he conquered a great military empire with a handful of some six hundred soldiers. The conquest of Mexico with this tiny army was mere child's play compared with another feat attempted by Cortes, namely, to keep his lawful wife, Doña Catalina Juarez Marcaida, and the delectable Marina in Coyoacan at the same time. After all, the conquest of Mexico was only a series of battles. At the end of a banquet at which Cortes and Doña Catalina both spoke what was on their minds, she suddenly died of 'asthma' — the kind of asthma which shows the marks of a man's fingers on the victim's throat. Doña Catalina is supposed to be buried in the old cemetery at Coyoacan — along with others who died of various kinds of asthma. The Cortes palace at Coyoacan has entirely disappeared. Within its walls the Aztec Prince Cuahutemoc was tortured to death in an attempt to make him reveal the hiding-place of the imperial treasures. Cortes was a nice fellow!

We saw the villa where he parked the lovely Marina, his Indian 'interpreter.' She was the most valuable interpreter in the history of the world. According to tradition, Marina was an Indian princess captured from another tribe and held as a hostage by the Aztecs. Probably Montezuma was out of cigars the day that Cortes called, so he gave him Marina. It was a fatal blunder. She grew to love her white captor and advised him in his campaigns, an important feature of which was the alienation of other Indian tribes from the Aztecs. It is a queer fact of history that few nations have ever conquered primitives without the help of other primitives. If the dark races of the world could have restrained their 'mads' at each other, there would be no white races. We should have been wiped off the face of the earth centuries ago. Had the Chinese and the Hindus and the Persians fought with Genghis Khan rather than against him, all Europe would by now have slant eyes and would be burning punk sticks. Just so the White Mountain Apaches beat old Geronimo when our army failed. We had to enlist the Crows to fight the Sioux for us.

We went to Cuernavaca, which, from Montezuma to Ambassador Morrow, has been the summer home of the famous. The present palace of the Governor was a summer palace built for Cortes; and from its splendid terraces he could watch the valley for uneasy dust-clouds that might give warning of an Aztec uprising. The hapless Maximilian, with Carlotta, spent some of his days at Cuernavaca playing at being a Mexican caballero in a silver saddle. The great Borda Gardens are here, too, and dim old churches.

One of our great days was the trip to Guadalupe — one of the great sacred shrines of the world. To the Mexican Indian it is what Mecca is to the Moslem. In almost every Catholic church in Western America you will find a picture of the Virgin of Guadalupe, painted on what looks to be a hide, but is supposed to be a blanket. It is a beautiful and interesting legend.

In the year 1531, an Indian peon named Juan Diego

was trudging over a bleak bare cactus hill when he became aware of strains of sweet music and found himself
enveloped in a strange, holy light. The Virgin appeared
to him and instructed him to carry word to the bishop of
that district that she desired to have a chapel built in her
honor at a place she pointed out to Juan Diego. The
bishop, skeptical of the peon's story, demanded proof.
Again the Virgin appeared to Juan Diego. She told him to
go to the top of the bare cactus hill and pick his blanket
full of roses as a token for the unbelieving bishop. Juan
Diego wonderingly climbed the hill, where he found a
miraculous garden of roses. Having picked his serape
full of blossoms, he carried them back and emptied the
blanket at the feet of the bishop. To his astonishment he
found that a beautiful picture of the Virgin had miracu-
lously imprinted itself on the serape. The blanket of
Juan Diego is still in the church at Guadalupe hanging
upon the high altar under glass. It was under this stand-
ard that the soldier-priest Miguel Hidalgo y Costilla led
the revolt against Spain in 1810.

Every year on December 12, a great celebration is
held in the old church on the anniversary of Juan Diego's
meeting with the Virgin. Indians make long pilgrimages
to be there. Guadalupe Hidalgo is a shabby little Mexican
town which is perpetually thronged with tourists —
American school-teachers with notebooks and horn-
rimmed glasses; rich tourists in fine cars; devout little
Mexicans in guarachas and soiled cotton drawers, who
have plodded over weary miles of country roads to pray
at the shrine and drink of the blessed waters. At the spot
where Juan Diego first saw the Virgin is a well that gushed
out from under her feet. Sometimes the water bubbles

benignly halfway up the well-curb, when the Virgin is pleased. When the Virgin is displeased, the water level drops. The day we were there, a sad little group of peasants were trying forlornly to fish up the blessed waters in a tin pail from a puddle in the wet mud at the bottom of the well.

It was in Guadalupe Hidalgo that the treaty of peace between Mexico and the United States was signed, the 'Treaty of Guadalupe Hidalgo' whereby Western America passed under the Stars and Stripes. It is a state secret that the United States intended to claim a great deal more than she got, but our emissary was feeling mellow that day.

At the top of the hill where Juan Diego found the roses is a chapel. Compared with most Mexican churches, it is small and unpretentious. Back of it lies an old cemetery with elaborate raised tombs much like the tombs in the cemeteries of New Orleans. The most notable grave is that of General Santa Anna — the 'Napoleon of the West.' He was one of the most extraordinary characters in the history of Mexico. He ordered the bloody massacre of the Alamo; then, in his underclothes, surrendered to Sam Houston at San Antonio. He was forever being defeated and disgraced, but always bobbed up smiling for new honors. No one else has ever had so romantic a hold on the imaginations of the Mexican people.

The climax of our Mexican adventures — and in a way the most momentous spiritual experience of my whole life — was the day we visited the pyramids at San Juan Teotihuacan. We rolled along through old city streets until the city fell away and the road led through pleasant fields. We stopped to take pictures of an old courtyard against the walls of which Morelos, the priest-general of the War of Independence, was executed by a firing squad.

Again we turned off a few miles to visit the magnificent old monastery of San Augustin. At one time it was half under water. You can still see the water-marks on the old Spanish doors. It must have been among the most splendid edifices of the New World. It is more like a palace than a religious retreat. It suggests the descriptions of the Alhambra, with its serene and beautiful patios now in ruins; cool dining-rooms with murals still on the walls, quaint stairways, cloisters, and the great vaulted church. San Augustin must have been very close to the heart of great wealth. Its cost must have been enormous; its luxuries imperial.

The pyramids of San Juan Teotihaucan stand on a wide level plain looking out toward Popocatepetl and Iztaccihuatl. You cannot but feel that these mountains had something to do with the selection of the site. These pyramids are among the mysteries of the world. We know exactly why the pyramids of Egypt were built and who built them. The story of the pyramids of Mexico is shrouded in mystery and darkness.

There are two large pyramids and several smaller ones. Originally they were surfaced with stone and had several terraces. One has been re-terraced by an archeologist, and, as usual, all the other archeologists say it is all wrong. It is assumed that one of the large pyramids was a temple to the sun; the second in size, a temple to the moon. The others are temples to the major planets. Astrologers of today read all kinds of meanings and symbols into the arrangement of these sacred mounds.

Near the pyramids is the excavated ruin of an old

Aztec house which is assumed to have been a residence for the high priests who came out for the ceremonies which were probably seasonal as the planets assumed certain positions. It is possible to identify with comparative clearness the purpose of the different rooms in this palace.

At the end of the majestic avenue of pyramids is a huge amphitheater which has been reconstructed from the mounds found there. It is an immense quadrangle surrounded by terraces, flat stone platforms approached by broad terraced steps. At one end of the quadrangle is a temple with steps leading to an altar. Exactly in the middle of the quadrangle is a high level platform like a giant prize-fight ring, with steps. In all probability the priests and kings gathered here for the great ceremonies of the Aztec year. It is considered probable that the sacrifices were made on the high altar and possibly sacred dances were held on the platform in the middle. One theory is that the different separated grandstands surrounding the quadrangle were set apart for the different tribes or castes. Whatever theory is advanced, all the other archeologists rise to point out that the theory is obviously wrong.

It is impossible to sit alone in that ancient place and not feel the world slip away... The Aztecs come again — the ancient splendor of Montezuma, the feathered cloaks, the glittering head-dresses of the warriors, the faltering approach of the beautiful boy to the altar, transported with religious ecstasy, shaken with mortal dread and terror, the flash of the black obsidian priest knife in the sun, the dreadful gurgling shriek of the victim bent back over the stone, the living heart still pulsing in the uplifted hand of the priest, the blood dripping down his arm and onto his linen and feathered robes, and at last the torn body bumping step by

step down the terraced throne, gathering scarlet stains
on pale flesh from the little river of blood...

Astronomers have announced that the place was built
according to the position of certain planets and thus
establish the age as two thousand five hundred years.
Near San Angel is a pyramid which shows signs of being
immeasurably older than that. At some forgotten period
of time a volcano belched out fire and brimstone and lava
all over this region. The ground is almost a lava pavement
for miles around. But the pyramid is not built of lava
rock. It is built of stone no longer to be found in that
vicinity. It is a fair conclusion that the pyramid was
built before the volcano spewed good building stone all
over the map — which would denote incalculable age.

Behind the temple is the most interesting wall in the
New World. It thrusts out, half-buried, from an em-
bankment, an elaborate stone bulwark, the front of a
building, intricately and beautifully carved with the
images of Aztec gods: fiercely scowling gods, serpent gods,
fat gods, Quetzelcoatl, Huitilopochtli, Tlahuizcalpante...
It stands to reason that back of this wall must be the remains of an ancient temple. It is now in process of careful
scientific excavation by trained archeologists. No other
country in the world is spending as much money on ruins
as Mexico.

The truth is that Mexico is reaching back to an ancient
spiritual heritage. The ancient cults of the Mayan, the
Aztec, and the Toltec are rising from the soil like a dark
miasma. The coming of the Spanish knights of Cortes
interrupted the life-flow of a great philosophy. Had the
Mayan been allowed to continue his civilization for another two hundred years, the jungles of Yucatan would

have produced an era more glorious than the Golden Age of Greece. Just so, the Aztec and the Toltec. These civilizations were overrun by various invaders and beaten down in their blood. But they did not die. Their thoughts and their spiritual impulses lived on. The most remarkable drama happening in the world today is the return of these ancient cultures to Mexico. The arts, the music, the drama, the cultures — even the religions — of those old Indian civilizations are stirring; are coming back to life. Daring young artists like Diego Rivera — terrific, crude, ungainly misshapen murals — they shake you with their power — savage splashes of color, devastating brutal strength. But they have not created a new art. They have merely reached down to lost and forgotten fires, to release something that has lain smoldering and steaming since the day of the Mayan temples and the human sacrifices of the Aztecs. Through the veneer of a sophisticated Moorish-Spanish culture, touched up by Hollywoodish spots, these old Indian mysteries are pushing their way into the soul of Mexico. Out of the mists of the past these old Indian races are coming back to finish their interrupted story. Whoever tries to deal with Mexico without reading this mighty soul drama is trying to judge an automobile by the paint on the hood; the nature of a tiger by the soft feel of the fur.

Who knows but that this temple into which they are now digging may not solve mysteries of ages; disclose hidden secrets. In a way this beautiful wall poking out from the side of a hill is symbolic of the search for the secret. The Aztec civilization has been a curtain which has hidden rather than revealed the past. There may or may not have been a Toltec race. Many latter-day scientists deny that such a race ever existed. They say that the Toltecs were merely a caste of architects and builders in the Aztec scheme of things. True or not, it is obvious that the Valley of Mexico was once occupied by a people who were possessed of high spiritual insight, to whom the occult was an open book. The Aztecs were a rough fighting people who came afterward. Just as some of the religious symbolisms of the American Indians have been reduced in significance to ghost dances, penitential tortures, and mud idols, so it is probable that the Aztecs, only half understanding what they found among the ruins of this previous civilization, tried to materialize the spiritual truths into something they could touch and feel. They dramatized half-perceived philosophic truths into funny-looking gods wiggling with snakes. Ideas that were probably purely abstract in the beginning were pepped-up with blood-fests in which the priests cut out the hearts of screaming victims. Aztec gods and the Aztec fondness for ritual and feather hats constitute a barrier to our search for the soul tracks of these earlier people.

It is a belief almost universal among the highly educated people of Mexico that this lost race was a marooned remnant of the population of the Lost Continent of Atlantis. Many startling things are found in the jungles of Mexico and Central America, relics that tie into the relics of the earliest Egyptian civilizations — some at least that are close cousins to the relics found in the seven-cities-deep ruins of Troy.

Nothing has been found thus far to prove the existence of Atlantis or to identify the 'mother race' of Mexico as Atlanteans. On the other hand, there is no clear reason to disprove it. During the last few years, the floor of the

Pacific Ocean has undergone great changes. Government vessels making ocean surveys have found bottom at six hundred feet where comparatively recent soundings showed depths of thirteen hundred feet. And *vice versa.* On the peaks of the High Sierras in California I have found ancient lagoons literally packed with prehistoric shellfish — more shells than earth. If continents can rise, they can also fall.

So, after all, the Aztecs and their pyramids are of not very great significance. We say that these young artists like Diego Rivera are, in their terrific and astounding murals, going back to the Aztecs. In truth, they are unconsciously trying to reach around the Aztecs to the wisdom and philosophy of an older people.

To me Mexico is a great seething crucible in which the plans of a mighty Destiny are being boiled out. In his book, 'The Race Life of the Aryan People,' Dr. J. P. Widney gives a hint of what this Destiny may be. In the mists before human history began to be written, the Aryan Race started from the high plateaus of Mid-Asia on a long trek. They were a herder people — a people of the grass. Driven on by some mysterious Destiny that they themselves did not understand, their impulse was always to press on toward the west. They founded empires and saw them fall. Then — over the ashes and the ruins — they pressed on toward the west. They founded a great empire in India — and pressed on. Built a mighty Greece and surged on to create the Roman Empire. Through its wreckage they crossed the Channel to lay the foundations of the British Empire.

The settlement of America showed how inexorable was their disciplined fate. It was written that they should never turn from their pathway around the earth. It was forbidden to them to leave the grass belts, the temperate zone. The Spanish landed far to the south — out of the accustomed avenue, the ordered route, of the Aryan trek — and the Spanish colonies decayed and perished. The French veered too far north into the snows of Canada — and their sovereignty crumbled and fell. The Teutonic Aryans kept to the grass belt. Although landing on bleak and forbidding shores, confronted by almost insurmountable mountains, they pressed on along the destined path and took root.

The last racial migration of the Aryan people was across the prairies to the Pacific Coast — the march of the covered wagons. The settlement of California was written in that far-forgotten day when the *Wanderlust* first seized those half-wild Aryan herders on the cold Mid-Asia mesas when man was young. The advice of Horace Greeley was plagiarized from the grunts of a half-wild ape-man who poked his hairy thumb toward the setting sun and said 'Come on.'

If it was our destiny to press always toward the west, then we have come to the end of the story. We are writing the last chapter. We have circled the globe. We stand at the shores of the Pacific and in the mist beyond, we see the wave-lashed shore of the home land from which we started to circle the earth. Our long trek has ended.

At about the same time that our flat-faced hairy ancestors were heading west from the Asian plateaus, another people were starting from the same place in the opposite direction. Their sealed orders from Destiny were to press ever toward the east — to hunt the rising sun while we walked toward the sunset. They also founded empires — empires of the Mayan, Toltecs, and the empires of the lost people.

We who trekked to the west developed into races of builders, fighters, explorers, machinists — people steeped and sunk in materialism. The people who pressed eastward became highly spiritualized — mystics, occultists. As we learned how to use mowing machines and guns, they perfected themselves in the knowledge of strange mysteries.

The history of races shows that, at intervals, the Aryans have turned south, and always a golden — if temporary — age of the world has resulted — the Golden Age of Greece, Imperial Rome, Spain of the treasure galleons...

The phosphorus of decay.

The Aryan races are turning southward again — spiritually if not physically. This sudden vogue for all things Latin that has seized America is not an accident. We have finished our mad race around the world. We have stopped with our forefeet stuck out stiff like steers driven into a fence. We have gone materially to a perilous point — until machinery threatens to destroy us like a Frankenstein monster. It is as though Providence had said: 'I have sent you around the world. You have seen everything. You have done everything. But you haven't had time to think about anything. Now sit down and meditate until you realize the meaning of what you have seen.'

In the ruins of these ancient Mexican civilizations — in the thought impulses that still linger there among these mysterious temples — are we perhaps to interpret our brash experiences? Have we — like the Aztecs — been sent to put life into the philosophies left by a wise and ancient people?

A new race is being developed in the world. We see advance scouts of it among our own flapper generations — daring, instinctive, intuitive. Just so in Mexico. Young men and women of advanced thought and high spiritual concept are digging down through the veneer of Spanish culture, down through the strong virile Indian civilizations, down through the Aztec arts and culture. They will not stop until they touch the thought impulses of the lost 'mother race.'

It has often been observed that the half-breed races of Mexico are dying out; that Mexico is taking up her heritage of strong Indian blood again. This is true. But the significance is deeper. Old Mother Mexico is whispering a lullaby to new races not yet born.

CHAPTER XXX

IN WHICH WE SAY GOOD–BYE

THE last night. Tomorrow we were to pull out. Three cars were to leave at daybreak by way of El Paso. The rest of us were to go north by train. El Norteño was to ride with the cars up the Laredo road. He was immeasurably proud. By telegraph we had arranged a job for him in Los Angeles. He was to be sent to school as a side issue. He was beginning to feel like a Yankee already. With obvious reluctance he took off his collegiate clothes and put on his old guaraches and sombrero.

Our highly intelligent immigration laws! It would have been all right had he been headed for California with every prospect of starving in the gutters. The fact that he had a good job ahead of him made him contract labor. He was with us in the hotel lobby when they came in from the consular office with the news.

I don't think he quite understood what it was all about. He only knew that, for some cruel reason, the light had been torn out of his soul. He took it like a soldier, standing very straight, with eyes shut down to a hard point and the color blanched from his face. Then suddenly he began to cry. His body was torn by sobs that seemed to be tearing his heart to pieces. I put my arm around his shoulders and made him sit down. He put his head down on my knee and cried until he could cry no longer. But we sat there for a long time. I remember how his long slim fingers ran up and down, ceaselessly sharpening the crease in my trousers.

Finally, one of the young engineers came in with a glowing inspiration. He was followed by another equally excited.

'Can the tears, Nicolas,' he said. 'We've got an idea. We will pull in at El Paso late at night. In the darkness we will sneak you across the border. Come on now, Old Top. We will be voting for you for mayor of Los Angeles some day.'

El Norteño dried his eyes carefully with his new handkerchief. He smiled at them tearfully, but slowly shook his head. 'If I can't go into the United States honorably, I don't want to go at all.'

The last time I saw El Norteño, he was sitting on a curb by the waiting automobiles which were packed and ready to start. Two engineers were sitting on each side of him on the curb and all five were crying.

THE END